The Right Combination

Unlocking Your Future Through Marketing

Don Levin & Todd Bothwell

authorHOUSE®

AuthorHouse™ LLC
1663 Liberty Drive
Bloomington, IN 47403
www.authorhouse.com
Phone: 1-800-839-8640

Published by AuthorHouse   04/23/2014

ISBN: 978-1-4969-0511-6 (sc)
ISBN: 978-1-4969-0510-9 (e)

Library of Congress Control Number: 2014907246

DEDICATION

"When you change the way you see things,
the things you see change."
—Wayne Dyer

To all of the agents that have made the decision to venture forth
into the future and put the past behind them. This book is for you.

"Success is not final,
Failure is not fatal,
It's about having the courage to continue on."
—Winston Churchill

CONTENTS

Final thoughts from two successful general agents/
managing partners who have shared professional life
experiences with their agents in the hope that we can
all reach more people each day and assist them in
avoiding financial failure while maintaining quality
health and long term care in retirement.

I

BELIEFS

"Here's to the crazy ones. The misfits. The rebels. The troublemakers. The round pegs in the square holes. The ones who see things differently. They're not fond of rules. And they have no respect for the status quo. You can quote them, disagree with them, glorify or vilify them. About the only thing you can't do is ignore them. Because they change things. They push the human race forward. And while some may see them as the crazy ones, we see genius. Because the people who are crazy enough to think that they could change the world, are the ones who do."
—Steve Jobs

"It's about converting a pipe dream to a pipe line."
—Todd Bothwell

Preface

"If you don't believe in yourself, how can you expect someone else to invest in your dreams?"
—Don Levin

When the two of us met a few years ago and began talking about marketing strategies, leadership styles, and our approaches as to how to foster growth in our individual agent's practices, we would have wonderful conversations leaving us wanting more.

While we would not often engage in conversations at home in our respective agencies, whenever we met again in subsequent conferences and company meetings, we would pick up almost exactly where we left off.

Because of the speed with which our industry is changing, and our company's response to these changes as an industry leader, we determined that rather than paying an exorbitant fee to a professional business coach who would coach us in generalities, we would begin to coach one another on a weekly basis, focusing these sessions on the specific challenges that we faced as General Agents. These 60 to 90 minute long sessions were designed to allow us to speak freely, share concerns, problems, best practices, and to truly serve as sounding boards to one another. While we both engage in a study group and participate in other group calls, this is solely our time. After several months we fell into a very comfortable rhythm on these calls, often sending one another e-mails containing formal agendas chocked full of points to ponder and to provide the framework for meaningful discussion. Through these calls it occurred to us, that perhaps we should be sharing this firsthand knowledge with others. Thus the book began.

Don's background is that of an attorney and military officer before becoming a sales leader in the insurance industry. Todd has had a highly successful career in sales and management over the past 36 years in insurance, investments and financial planning. We grew up in different places with different academic careers. So how did two guys with such divergent backgrounds come together to write this book? It is because of our passion as servant leaders for supporting our agents and helping them grow their businesses by expanding their spheres of influence to include working with other financial and legal professionals with client books of business. We find great self-actualization in watching agents, both new and veteran, attain new heights in professional achievement. We fervently believe that the key to solving the long term care crisis facing the American public, particularly the Baby Boomer generation, is to reach as many people as possible with a holistic approach that hopefully will keep individuals from outliving their money and/or enduring the ravages of long term care expenses. With the obsolescence of direct mail and the abundance of other less efficient methodologies, we believe the key to reaching these people rests in the development of strategic alliances and professional partnerships with other professionals who enjoy a fiduciary relationship with their clients.

The methodologies that we will discuss are far beyond theory as both of us have lived them and established them as tried and true practices that are replicable by those who are willing to leave their comfort zone and embrace the concept of being a little *uncomfortable.*

So thank you for the confidence and/or curiosity that led to you to pick up this book. A number of you have been asking us to reduce these thoughts to paper, so with further ado, here it is. It is our hope that you will find it packed with proven best practices that you can embrace and start using today to recruit more qualified professional partners and to seamlessly mesh with other organizations to build mutually profitable relationships. This IS the future delivery mechanism for the services we have to offer to our clients.

As Dhirubhai Ambani summed it up, "If you don't build your dream, someone else will hire you to build theirs."

Don Levin

Todd Bothwell

CHAPTER 1

Why Should I Read This Book

"We shall have no better conditions in the future if we are
satisfied with all those which we have at present."
—Thomas Edison

The alarm goes off on Monday and we are excited about going
to work! Are you? I know very few people who as children wanted
to be insurance producers, and yet here we all are striving to be the
best and brightest product specialist in our local marketplace. Today,
being the best and the brightest in our business also requires us to
be entrepreneurial in our thinking and our actions. As Edison stated
above, we can't accept the status quo like an employee or manager if
we want something different or better. It is up to us as entrepreneurs
to look at the status quo and determine how we need to change it so
as to influence the desired future outcome. Our industry continues to

evolve with new product, new underwriting, new pricing, and the need to market our message differently as well. If you are serious about your business, we believe that this book will both shorten and accelerate your learning curve and propel your practice to new heights.

Have you thought about what your current career is all about and the degree of difference you make in the lives of your clients? As Joe Jordan has noted in his own work, we have the opportunity to truly live a life of significance as we serve our clients and their families. Take a minute and think about the number of clients and their families that you have assisted either with a death benefit check on a life insurance policy you may have sold to a young couple "just in case" something happens, or the phone call you receive from the spouse or a child of a long term care policyholder when they are overwhelmed by the enormity of having to become a caregiver to a loved one. We make a huge difference in their lives! However, we can't make this difference in their lives unless we first meet with them. Why should you read this book? Simple: so that you get in front of more people. We have spent the majority of our adult lives working to this single goal and want to share the secrets that have made us modestly successful at what we do. We don't profess to know all the answers or how to walk on water, but we have been doing this long enough to figure out where the rocks are located.

> The key to this business is being in front of more people. Some of these people will become clients while others will become professional associates that will *put you in front* of people with whom *they* have a relationship, while others will become centers of influence providing you with the right combination to unlock and open even more doors.
>
> —Don Levin

Still not convinced that you should continue reading? As previously stated, this book is all about how to get in front of more people. Some of these people will become clients while others will become professional associates that will *put you in front* of people with whom *they* have a relationship, while others will become centers of influence providing you with the right combination to unlock and open even more doors.

For this reason, this book presents our unique experiences book in marketing and branding your business. It can't be because the world has changed so much, and continues to change on an accelerating basis. The reality of selling long term care insurance and ancillary products has changed significantly with the ending of the direct mail and mass lead generation systems. Think about all the changes you have witnessed in your own life thus far. Computers, personal computers, lap top computers, the iPad. The brick phone, the flip phone, the Smart phone. From the flip phones that greatly resemble the then-fictional communicators of *Star Trek* to the smart phones and iPads that would even have Mr. Spock marveling at them, all of which that harness more memory and energy than some of the largest computers ever previously constructed, it is all about the change that is coming at us faster and faster and in ever growing waves. Further evidence of this would be how going to the local movie theater was replaced with the ability and option of staying home through the utilization of Blockbuster, which in turn was replaced by Netfix, and certainly there will come a time when Netflix goes by the wayside.

It is about instant communications and gratification. Snail mail has yielded to e-mail. Texting is the new wave of the advertiser. How often do we hear someone say, "How did we ever exist without a cell phone?" Easy, you carried a roll of dimes and used the pay phone when that new-fangled pager went off indicating that someone needed to communicate with you immediately.

Change is something to be embraced if we are to thrive in this new world. For us, it is imperative that we change along with the world around us if we are going to continue to service the clients who so badly need what we have to offer. If you are reading this book and have clients who rely on your advice, then you will find the answers of how to re-tool your business going forward. For many years, the reigning school of thought for sales leaders was to insure that you were taking care of that 20% of the sales force that was accounting for 80% of the business. We believe that if you are reading this book, particularly as a new member of the industry, then you are part of the *other* 80% that will virtually change the world of sales. If as you read this book you should agree that it is what you need to be doing, and set your mind to doing it, you <u>will</u> be part of the industry's top tier of producers.

Many years ago Robert F. Kennedy said, "Some men see things as they are and say why, I dream of things that never were and say why not." While he was speaking of life in this country on a far grander scale, the same can be said for us in our chosen careers as well. Think big, Dream Big, and don't be afraid of doing something different. Get out of your comfort zone and embrace the idea of being uncomfortable in the short term.

For those who may be too young to remember RFK, let us express it in the words of Disney's Aladdin, when he said it's "a whole new world." This whole new world is full of selling opportunities on a scale that we have never yet experienced; a marketplace growing faster than we can service it.

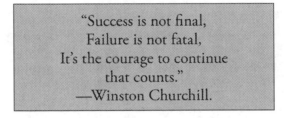

"Success is not final,
Failure is not fatal,
It's the courage to continue
that counts."
—Winston Churchill.

This is not Marketing for Dummies, or a general 'how to' book, but rather the best practices of fifty plus years of *specific* experience of two sales leaders committed to the success of their agents, who have also been on the street just like you, attempting to become known as product experts in their local market. Our combined experiences allow us to share with a high degree of confidence what is in the minds of the advisors that you will be meeting with in hopes of making them your strategic partners. We know what will cause them to shrink back from the relationship ranging from fear of losing clients to looking incompetent or lacking in the eyes of their clients. We will share with you how to overcome these as well as many other objections. We have lived in many different markets around the country and have discovered many universal truths that we will also share with you. We are rainmakers dedicated to working hard on behalf of our agents in an effort to penetrate these various and sundry markets. We know that the old adage that you learn more from your failures rather than your successes is true, and suffice to say that we have learned a whole lot in those fifty years, and there is no need for you to earn your degree at the school of Hard Knocks as we have done. Just as parents want their children to learn from their mistakes rather than experiencing their own, we know that you are all going to have to experience your own series of trials and errors. And while it is sometimes good for the child to fall and skin their knee, we also know that we can't allow them to touch the hot stove or walk into traffic with the associated dire consequences. For this reason we hope that you will want to work smarter and not harder, while growing your individual practices. What we offer you in these pages is a blueprint of how to build lasting fruitful relationships that in fact get you in front of more people.

Marketing to us is pretty simple. Do it, do it right, and do it right now. It is not easy, but it is a simple process. It requires us to possess a certain mindset and embracing that marketing is a lifestyle and not merely an event. It is not easy to work tirelessly in this endeavor day in and day out, but we know the sweet taste of success that accompanies the formation of a relationship that really works to the betterment of everyone, most notably the clients. We have an associate who is now semi-retired from our industry and has a retirement income in excess of a quarter million dollars per annum. To meet him is to talk with a very unassuming person who in his own estimation is very boring. Why is he now retired and enjoying the fruits of his labors? Marketing. Our friend discovered very early on in his career that the key to his future success was to turn all of his clients and their circles of influence into his personal marketers. While others continued to view our business as a transactional-based system, he fostered his own personal relationship-based system, and the rest we say is History. As evidenced by our friend, proper marketing will in fact provide you the right combination to your own future success.

Unlocking the door of your success begins right now if you turn the page . . .

Chapter Tumblers—Take-Aways:

 Marketing will unlock your future

 There is an infinite market of professionals with whom to partner.

 Been there, done that . . . it's all about getting out there and doing it!

CHAPTER 2

Starting the Process

"The first step toward success is taken when you refuse to be a captive of the environment in which you first find yourself."
—Mark Caine

When Monday morning comes, and an agent who is committed to marketing calls the office and asks, "What should I be doing to grow my business today, this week, and for the rest of the year," it forces us to really ponder an answer that would be worthy of Solomon.

Where *does* an agent start the process to working with one or more Professional Partners? It begins by cultivating the zeal of a missionary and recognizing that we have an incredibly important message that needs to be shouted from the roof tops. This passion, sincerity, and conviction must be heartfelt and if it is, will therefore be communicated to the person you are seeking to make a professional partner. You must sincerely believe that you have solutions to a retirement planning issue many people are unaware or in denial of, and at all costs work to insure that you are not overwhelmed by the denial and negativity that you will encounter.

We believe that people have an easier time talking to people with whom they can talk common industry slang and truly appreciate the other person's point of view. As a result of this, you will enjoy a decided advantage when you seek out financial advisors, wealth managers, estate planning attorneys, and elder law attorneys, if you can speak their common language. Do some research on the profession of the person you are going to meet; go to their website if they have one (most do these days) and find out what you can about them personally, professionally, and regarding their philosophical dispositions. You will be better able to relate to them and their perspective, thus allowing you to put yourself in their shoes, which is critical when you are trying to affiliate with another professional partner.

Work to your own sweet spot. By this we mean, if your background is in teaching, nursing, special education, day care, financial services, ministry, auto sales, or if you owned your own business, etc., your initial reaching out to others to cultivate additional centers of influence should be in one of these spheres of influence where you already have developed relationships and people can relate to you and you to them. After these humble beginnings, you may then branch out and be in a position to tell people what you do for a living, e.g. the elevator speech, that you have heard so much about. For example, if you were a nurse in your previous life you may not want to walk into a CPA firm on your first couple of visits. Get your confidence up by approaching other nurses and begin the practice of relaying your message about the benefits of working with you, your support system, and company by approaching other people who have similar experiences.

The focus for years has been to approach other professionals and help their clients by working their book of business and see if we could be the one to give their clients the solution of long term care insurance. This has met with only mediocre success over the years. The key now is to focus on building the *relationship* with the other professional. We do this by meeting with them and, as in the home interview with clients, listening to what they offer clients, what makes them unique to the market place; and how they view their role in influencing and shaping their clients' lives by asking them the same type of open-ended questions that we would typically pose to our clients. Stay true to your principles and paradigms. You want to know what has made them successful and by listening to that train of thought you can position your offering so that it works into or integrates with their practice and goals.

There are many avenues to take and you should not limit yourself to only one or two; try to incorporate as many as you can each week into the marketing of your business. Eventually once you go through your warm contacts you will want to head to the internet and start searching for other professionals with whom to work, at which time you will have to make a category decision as to where to start. Do you want to meet with health insurance agents, CPAs, attorneys, life insurance agents, benefits brokers, real estate agents, doctors' groups, property and casualty owners, or financial planners?

Try to choose a business that you can service relatively easily and conversely serves you. Stay close to your home or office so you can work smart and not hard. Depending on your geography you can start with the zip codes close to you and identify those professionals first and then make your approach whether it is by calling them or stopping by to get acquainted with their offering or service. Build the business you want with the people you have common interests with, so that they will in turn want to do business with you. Join networking groups in your area where you work and live. Join associations that have a common purpose of protecting people, e.g. their incomes, assets, providing high quality care, preserving multiple generations and futures.

Chapter Tumblers—Take-Aways:

 Work your known markets.

 Believe you are the expert and bring Value.

 Design a business that will serve you while you serve others.

CHAPTER 3

What's In It for Me?

> "The difference between a succcessful person and others is not a lack of strength, not a lack of knowledge, but rather a lack of will."
> —Vince Lombardi

As basic a question as any element of Abraham Maslow's Hierarchy of Needs is the proverbial "what's in it for me?" or 'WIIFM' hereafter, that everyone asks when encountering a new situation or opportunity. As we apply the WIIFM to the question of why it is critical to engage in marketing to professionals the answers becomes quite clear in that agents who do so will enjoy:

- Greater independence
- Greater Control
- Greater referral flow

- Better time management
- Improved balance in and quality of life
- More opportunities to grow your business
- Easier appointments to set, and to close
- More qualified people with whom to work
- Greater retention of clients
- The ability to 'borrow trust' from the relationship that your new strategic partner has with their clients which exponentially advances the client relationship that you in turn will enjoy.
- The ability to sell multiple products to clients (assuming that your strategic partner does not engage in the sale of these products).
- Opportunity. We are only scratching the surface of the market potential. There is a flood of baby boomers that need to talk to us. 79 million Baby Boomers, turning age 65 at the rate of 10,000 per day for the next 17 years, and then the Gen-X'ers who are an 84 million member cohort.
- Networking allows us to leverage ourselves by working through our strategic partners' new and existing clients while essentially offering them a turn-key marketing system by which to offer their clients long term care planning and the accompanying insurance. We'll look at this value added in chapter 4.
- Professional Partner Production (P^3) is liberating and allows you to truly control your own business. You became Independent contractors to be independent, not dependent; an entrepreneur, not a cubical dweller making cold calls.
- P^3 keeps you where you want to be, i.e. you can build the market that you want in the market you want. With leads, you have to go where they are!
- Since you don't have to pay for the [direct mail generated] lead any longer, this new source of clientele can virtually be cost free to you.

In light of all these obvious wins, why are agents still reticent to market themselves, build their own brand name in the local market, and really cash in on these "sales waiting to happen"? We have captured some anecdotal data and comments from our agents over the years, and share it with you now for your edification. It is in no way intended to be all inclusive.

- **Fear.** How do you have a rational discussion about something that is inherently irrational? When our children were younger and attending school we would encourage them to always put forth their best efforts. This included preparing for exams, completing assignments on time, and approaching these tasks with confidence. On one occasion I asked my son on the eve of a big exam how he felt and whether he was afraid of the exam, he quickly responded, "why should I be afraid? I am prepared." So it is with marketing. It is nothing more than preparation and execution.

- **Laziness.** "I just don't want to do it. Utilizing company, agency, or district generated leads is just plain easier!" Boy, if we had a nickel for every time that we heard that one, we would have a mountain of nickels! Unless you are the owner of a well-established business and have a great staff and management team, which allows you to 'coast' or to semi-retire on the job, it is extremely hard if not impossible to be 'lazy' in your own business. 'Entrepreneurial' and 'lazy' are for the most part completely mutually exclusive terms.

- **Comfort.** Agents are unwilling to leave their comfort zone or as we have heard time and time again, "I'm just not comfortable doing it." That, at least is an honest answer with which we can work. The key to success in this new market is all about displaying a willingness to be uncomfortable and to think and act outside the six sides of the box.

- **Attitude.** Our agents are probably tired of hearing about attitude, but it has never been more important. Attitude and belief fuel our actions. Congruence is how we define the manner in which we approach our tasks and is a reflection of our attitude. So what is your mindset towards marketing? What is your view of selling—is it a noble endeavor or do you feel 'dirty' for having to accept the fact that you are in fact a salesperson? How do you feel about the products you sell? Do you embrace long term care planning as a key to the financial success of our clients as they continue to live their lives and hopefully not outlive their money? How do you view your own abilities? Are you competent and confident? Are your values in line with the vision and mission of your agency? Do you have a comprehensive plan that reflects your personal goals and objectives for your business?

- **Museum.** "As long as leads are flowing, I'm not going to worry about building up my own sources of agent generated business." What can be said about the short-sighted nature of this statement? The days of abundance in company generated direct mail leads are long since gone and/or ineffective. Can anyone spell dinosaur?

- **Discomfort.** "In my past careers I have never had to market before; this lack of experience in actually marketing myself makes me uncomfortable." Again, the key to success in today's Baby Boomer/Gen-X oriented market is all about building your brand even if it means doing new things that may make you uncomfortable.
- **Confidence.** "Lack of experience in long term care insurance, life, and annuities, makes me reticent to go into the market place and promote myself as an expert." This statement sounds like a cry for help and a real testimonial for joint work and mentoring. We both believe that you don't have to have all the answers or right words, but rather only 3-4 pertinent questions. More on those topics in future chapters as well.

So again, why do it? Why engage in marketing? What is in it for you? Everything. It is nearly the difference between night and day. It used to be that marketing was something that you did to supplement your lead business; now it is all about using leads as seed money to unlock your own marketing business!

> "It isn't the smartest or the
> strongest species that survive,
> it's the most adaptable."
> —Charles Darwin

Chapter Tumblers—Take-Aways:

  It's about independence, not dependence.

  The world is changing . . . . Are you?

  Discomfort and fear can be building blocks if you embrace change.

CHAPTER 4

What's In It for me . . . the Professional Partner?

"A successful man is one who can lay a firm foundation
with the bricks that others have thrown at him."
—David Brinkley

Just as it is important to discover what is motivating the client to investigate long term care insurance as a potential solution to their long term care planning needs and financial strategies, it is equally important to discover the WHY a professional partner may be seeking to work with you! Is it to protect their clients and their families? Is it to safeguard this own professional cash flow? Is it to be construed as an alternate income stream for the professional in what might be a down market? Is it to ward off potential liability down the road for when these clients go in to a care situation that warrants the liquidation of their assets and they or their heirs may be less than pleased and initiate legal action against the professional? This last option has become far more prevalent as the courts have been very critical of both the advice a professional does and *does not* tender to a client! Are the heirs going to find your business card in the Safe Deposit Box? If so, will they write you a thank you note or a legal complaint?

In any event, don't be in any great hurry to forge a relationship with another professional. What? Turn down the opportunity to add someone to my network of strategic partners? Yes. The reason is that if it is not a good fit, you will waste valuable time and resources pursuing a relationship that will not bear fruit or could even be counterproductive in terms of your brand development.

For example, if this professional does not personally own a long term care policy himself/herself, odds are against him being a strong advocate of the product with his clients. To this end, even if he recommends it to his clients, and doesn't own it himself when asked by a client about his own coverage, odds are there is not going to be a sale made unless the professional does not qualify for the coverage which in itself becomes a very strong positive message to the client as to why they need to buy now.

In the event the professional does not own a policy, the next step is to suggest that he and his spouse sit with you for a home interview under the guise of learning exactly what you will be doing with their clients. If this interview takes place and they opt to purchase a plan, then you have hit the mother lode! There is no greater advocate than a convert.

If they refuse to sit with you, the word 'next' should flash through your mind, because this dog is not going to hunt!

For the most part, you are going to discover that these professionals care about their clients as much as we care about ours, and they have a great affinity to protecting them from forces that can harm them. As a result of this concern they are going to want to address the issue of long term care with their clients. They may very well already be doing it in the course of annual interviews. Our experience has been that while they care enough to broach the subject, they simply lack the skill set and/or knowledge that you possess to adequately *educate* the clients and assist them in making an informed decision that results in action, and/or are at capacity individually or as an office team to add anything more to their menu.

Some professionals you encounter may be suspicious of your intentions. They may have been inundated by other insurance professionals offering an array of products to their clients. Some may be leery of you, and view you as an interloper only interested in gaining access to their book of business. On this point be very clear; we are <u>not</u> interested in their books of business. We don't want their client list or to engage in cold calls that we find frustrating and more often than not, the client finds aggravating and may cause harm to their existing relationship. Rather, we want to offer the professional a turn-key marketing system by which <u>they</u> can bring the protections afforded by a long term care insurance policy to their clients by making <u>you</u> a trusted member of his or her staff. This is a totally different mindset that we have found to be very disarming, if not darn right shocking, to the professional. Try it, it works, you can be part of their team.

If you meet a professional who is simply in it for the money, we call this person the mercenary. That *may* work for you, but you have to insure from the beginning the degree of their commitment. Later, when we talk about how we present the professional with the *opportunity* to *earn* up to 50% of the sale, we have to know that they and their staff are going to fully engage in our newly formed partnership and not merely pay lip service to it.

For those who are simply looking to expand the scope of their practice with additional product offerings that is okay as well. The key is to insure that they understand that unlike disability or a Medicare insurance product this is decidedly not a commodity sale. While some clients will choose to buy purely on the recommendation of the professional, in the vast majority of cases if they do not, in their heart of hearts, feel the need for this additional insurance platform, they are not going to buy. For this reason you must insure that the professional is 'trained up' to understand just how important a LTCI policy is to the overall plan that he/she is preparing for their client and they must sincerely believe that it is an integral part of this plan.

Just as with our clients, the professional must recognize and *feel* the NEED, the URGENCY, and recognize the VALUE of our product if this is going to be a viable partnership.

If you are working with a professional who is not life and health insurance licensed and therefore ineligible to receive a portion of generated commissions, you may be able to offer them other forms of non-compensation such as the sponsorship of client appreciation events, referral events, educational workshops, etc., the cost of which you bear in exchange for the opportunity to educate their clients. We'll share more on this later as well.

Like everything else we are talking about in this book, none of it is going to work for you unless you make the commitment to becoming a full-fledged entrepreneur. As such, you will engage in marketing, networking, and prospecting as these activities become less an event and more a way of life.

Chapter Tumblers—Take-Aways:

 It is critical to acknowledge the goals and objectives of the Professional Partner.

 As with our clients, it is all about creating Need, Urgency and Value.

 It has to be the right relationship . . . don't be afraid to say 'next' while marketing to professionals.

CHAPTER 5

The Pregame Warm Up

"You can have all the business you want if you are honest
with yourself, write up a plan, and really go after it."
—Todd Bothwell

The very foundation of our business is belief and activity. As such,
the first decision that you need to make for yourself is just how serious
you are about cutting the umbilical cord, and truly liberating yourself
by pursuing a network of professional partners and *freeing* yourself
from the dependency of any company generated lead program.

With that decided the next step is determining your natural
market and any potential target markets in which you wish to align
yourself. We'll define and discuss this later.

The following is a series of questions that you must answer for
yourself:

- Exactly what geographical area do you want to work in over the next 5-10 years?
- How far are you willing to travel to secure and continue servicing your partner's clients?
- How many hours a week do you want to dedicate to this work with partners' clientele? 40-50-60-70 hours per week?
- Are you going to work 5 or 6 days a week?
- Are you going to work evenings and/or take Saturday appointments?
- What product or products do you want to specialize in?

The good news is that there are many, many, many partners with whom you can align your practice. You have the benefit of not having to work with any professional partner with whom you do not share similar values. In fact, we would recommend that it is absolutely critical to the success of the partnership that you share common beliefs and personalities. This shared ground will enable you to truly help people. You should ideally also share the same paradigms regarding the transferring of risk, varying selling styles, as well as the other beliefs that have led you to dedicate your time/life to the cause you have chosen. As noted, you do not have to work with every financial partner you meet. If the chemistry is not to your liking, simply take the attitude that one of our agent's displays on his car's license plate: NEXT! That being said, ask yourself another set of questions:

- What type of person do you enjoy working with?
- Can you see yourself working with this person for endless hours?
- Are you going to work with health insurance agents, CPAs, attorneys, life agents, institutions, financial planners, or all of the above?
- Do you want to pursue sole proprietors, institutions, large firms, medium sized firms, or smaller offices?

With the above profile of your desired partner established, you can now start the research on your targeted professional partner market.

- Are you going to pursue clients in their 30's; 40's, 50's, or 60's?

- How many clients does the firm need to have to keep you in 8-10-12 appointments per week throughout the year? Are you intending to work with multiple firms? What size client base does each of them need to have in order for you to achieve your desired appointment level?

- Do you have a junior agent or case manager within your agency that you can bring in to assist with the paperwork and tracking the policies to issue in the first year?

- Is this going to be the same person in year two that is going to help you with the excess sales appointments you can't keep up with by yourself?

- Do you prefer to work within any particular cohort or target markets such as people who are athletes; people of a certain faith, male or female preference, and other filters you may want to utilize on the search engine request.

With this further refinement, you may continue on a macro search and start searching the internet web for your criteria of firms in your desired geographical area. For example, a multi-partner CPA firm in the greater Kansas City metro area that in turn belongs to the American Society of Certified Public Accountants and specializes in individual and small business tax planning with an emphasis on financial planning may be your desired sweet spot. You can further refine the search by adding the zip code and start winnowing down your search until you identify several firms with which to begin conversations. Keep in mind that building a practice like this is a lot like the game of dominoes. When you successfully affiliate with your first firm they will become part of your marketing team and share you with their fellow professionals, unless they take the opposite tact and become territorial in their desire to keep you all for themselves. In either case, it is a tremendous victory for you!

Depending on the nature of the professional practice with which you wish to affiliate, you also have to ask yourself the following question:

- What time of year is the best time to approach a firm about a partnership? For example, if the professional partner has any industry deadlines, you need to be sensitive to these factors, and manage your marketing year around these deadlines. To this end, CPAs have April and October deadlines for personal returns. Medicare Advantage agents have open enrollment between October and December. Don't waste your time because they will be too busy to see you. Likewise, Health Benefit professionals will be swamped in December and January dealing with new enrollment year coverage.

Once you define what market you want to work with, all you need to do is work your plan each and every week. You can't dabble in this marketing venture; it requires total commitment on your part. It is hard but rewarding work. If you find yourself hedging for any reason, talk yourself back into the marketing plan fulltime. Fear and procrastination will be your two biggest self-made enemies. Those who overcome those two enemies will win and take market share from everyone else.

The market is huge so do not let it overwhelm you; just focus on it one day at a time, and remember that finding that <u>one</u> special professional relationship can keep you busy for a long time.

Chapter Tumblers—Take-Aways:

 Do your homework—there are no shortcuts.

 Take a hard look at your filtering questions.

It is a simple business model; don't confuse simple with easy.

CHAPTER 6

Designing a Guerilla Marketing Plan

"You have to learn the rules of the game. And then you
have to learn to play better than anyone else."
—Albert Einstein

Whether you are the newest of agents or the most experienced veteran, your need for a comprehensive marketing plan is the same. The two resources that you have to draw upon are also the same: Money and Time. Most agents never seem to have enough of the former [no matter how long they have been in the business or how large their renewal stream may be] and are usually reticent to invest the latter for any number of reasons. These reasons may range from a perceived lack of time, expertise, interest, to desire, or vision.

It is important for you to recognize that whether you are a part of an agency or purely on your own, you are a business owner and to be successful, you must be a true entrepreneur.

With that as a premise, we begin encouraging our agents during the selection process to start building their brand so that when people think of long term care in your geographical area that they will instantly think of you. Our goal is to help you build your brand so effectively that your name is synonymous with your favorite product.

To achieve this, it is necessary to get out there, press the flesh, and to be okay with being the 'new person in the Chamber of Commerce,' and to introduce yourself to fellow members, listening to what they have to say, but insuring that they know what you do for a living. That is how one goes about building their personal brand.

So, that sounds pretty straight forward, but how does one really get started? Our suggestion is for you to reach out to your agency's leadership. They will often be able to school you in very short order on how to approach and evaluate the local chambers of commerce in your area. You don't want to join it if there are already six professionals offering the same products and services that you do. If they are well established, you may be wasting both valuable time and money in this endeavor. Move on to the next opportunity.

Your manager should also be in a position to advise you on what sort of co-op funding programs, if any, are available in order to stretch your own marketing dollars.

One of our new agents has hit the ground running, has partnered with a slightly more senior agent and together they have joined eight chambers of commerce together and are doing an excellent job of guerilla marketing. Like partisans who operate under the cloak of darkness, they are creating an all-out assault on the local chambers in order to get near-instant name recognition. Both have ambitions of building their own respective teams of agents that they can leverage themselves by pre-establishing these business to business relationships.

Besides chambers of commerce, what else can an agent do? Visit health care and long term care facilities in your area. Get to know the administrators and workers. Offer to participate in family day/night and to conduct educational seminars for the family members of those in residence. These family members are often living the nightmare associated with long term care and would be a natural audience for you and your products. Visiting these facilities and establishing a presence in them will give you enhanced credibility with your other clients.

Become active in community volunteer organizations such as United Way, the Alzheimer's Association, Muscular Dystrophy, March of Dimes, or any other charity that has significance to you or your family. These require longer commitments and will not ordinarily bear fruit at the beginning, but sometimes you will be surprised. Do though be prudent with your time and spend it wisely. Always keep your goal in front of you and remember why you are there.

BNI® (Business Network International) Groups are also a source of referrals, but since membership is typically limited to only one such group, it is imperative that you are extremely discerning when determining which you will join. If you can't find one that is a good fit, then perhaps creating your own is the way to go. This will allow you to hand pick those professionals that will most likely be of mutual benefit to one another.

Health Fairs, Community Fairs and Community "Days" where there is high volume of foot traffic are also great places to start building your brand. Have a table with balloons, table cloth, brochures, candy, and other giveaways that will draw people to your booth. Don't be afraid to engage people in conversation and to "wow" them with your super slick elevator talk about what you do and the *value* that you provide to your clients. As alternative, just attend these events as a participant; network and market yourself to the vendors and the other attendees.

Guerilla marketing as we are fond of calling it usually requires only a modest investment of cash and is almost always demanding of your time. The rewards however make these pursuits well worth the effort.

For fear of sounding like a Nike commercial, just get out there and do it. Have fun, and remember that nobody knows what you know, and how you can be of help to the people around you. "Guerilla" marketing is not monkey business.

Chapter Tumblers—Take-Aways:

 Build your brand at the grass roots level.

 Be selective and discerning while also realistic.

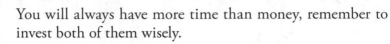 You will always have more time than money, remember to invest both of them wisely.

II

INTRODUCTIONS

"We didn't all come over on the same ship,
but we are all in the same boat."
—Bernard Baruch

CHAPTER 7

Getting Started with Introductions

"If we did all the things that we were capable
of, we would astound ourselves."
—Thomas Edison

So where does the professional relationship begin? Where do we begin our marketing efforts aside from networking events? How do we obtain those warm introductions which open doors to friends, family, neighbors, and co-workers as well as to the professionals? In addition to the marketing previously discussed, many of these opportunities can begin at the Point of Sale with a referral.

Now we know that "referral" has become both an ambiguous and less than socially embraced term and for that reason we are going to prefer the term "introduction."

I had a Health Benefits Broker who not only was willing to *refer* me, but actually *preferred* to make a *warm introduction* by accompanying me to the appointment which he would set with another professional, someone within his own sphere of influence (he is a Rotarian), or one of his own clients. It was wonderful.

For most of you reading this book, introductions will be obtained from clients whom you have sold a long term care insurance policy and/or another product, a center of influence, or professional partner.

So how do you really get started in the introduction business? It starts in the Home Interview. Plant introduction seeds throughout the interview from the time you begin warm up until you are solidifying the sale. Be a good listener.

> Introductions can become
> habit forming . . . but only
> if you ask for them!

The best Introductions habit that exists is thinking ahead of time about exactly what you want to ask for when you meet a client, a potential ambassador, or center of influence. This requires preparation and for you to be a bit strategic rather than flying by the seat of your pants. At the start of each week look at what meetings you have coming up and ask yourself: "What would I love to ask this person to help me with when I meet with them?" Do you know all the potential doors this person could open? Probably not! With repetition, your creativity juices kick in and will help you expand your comfort zone.

Once you know how to get quality Introductions, avoid the common trap of staying in your 'new and improved' comfort zone. Avoid asking for the same thing you did a year ago (unless that's your ideal client). Keep stretching yourself with more ambitious requests.

Like everything else in our business, it is important to be consistent and to track the results of your Introductions' solicitations. We realize that none of these habits sound very attractive, and few people strong in sales or business development have the patience for even important detail and planning work like tracking.

The key reasons for you to change and track better:

a) To better nurture your Introductions sources
b) Persistence pays
c) Many business decisions take months—like an executive carve-out or small group plan.

Start modestly and just track the Introductions you receive. At least then you are revisiting the opportunities and contact information. Then track how often you are asking and the quality of your requests. This may need more than one category—bread and butter business versus the elephant hunting. Some of this is embarrassingly simple: if you want more, ask for more and ask for bigger. Your numbers won't lie!

Being human involves not being perfect. So when you get a bit sloppy down the road, and either forget to ask, or are too intimidated to ask for an Introduction, pick yourself up, dust yourself off, and ask again! This is a lifetime skill and you can only get better over time. Like a muscle, your Introductions requesting mechanism must be exercised regularly. It will get bigger and stronger, but only when you keep using it! The alternative is that it will atrophy and eventually die.

Keep an eye on whether your business is trending up because of what you're asking for, and determine which habit makes the biggest difference for you.

Chapter Tumblers—Take-Aways:

 Ask for Introductions daily so that doing so becomes Habit.

Track your results. Where performance is measured, it always improves.

 Your words don't need to be perfect; you just need to keep asking

CHAPTER 8

A Simple Formula for Introductions

"The three great essentials to achieve anything worthwhile are,
first, hard work; second, stick-to-itiveness; third, common sense."
—Thomas Edison

With most things, timing is everything. As some of you are jumping into the water and attempting to build the self-generated portion of your practice around Introductions, keep in mind that there are times to *promote* Introductions and other times to *ask* for Introductions. Clearly, this is where the "art" of Introductions comes into play. For those of you who have participated in the Introductions Advantage Program® by Bill Cates, you know the simple answer to when to ask for Introductions is "When value has been delivered and value has been recognized."

Many people have asked Bill for a formula for when to ask for Introductions, so they can make asking a habit. Bill has given this formula out in past Introductions Minutes®, but it bears repeating from time to time.

First meeting with a new client:

1. Deliver great value. The easiest way to do this is to keep the spotlight on the client and to exceed his or her expectations.
2. Ask a value-seeking question. "We've covered a lot of ground in this first meeting. Tell me, what stands out as the most valuable or important part of this meeting?"
3. Plant a seed for Introductions. (Such as, "Don't keep me a secret" or any of the many other ways to promote Introductions.)

Second meeting with a new client (especially if you did not close the sale the first time):

1. Deliver great value. Remember, we have *knowledge* that the client needs. Add *professionalism* to that, and we become a very great value to the client.
2. Ask a value-seeking question.
3. Plant a seed for Introductions.

Third meeting with a new client (could be policy or plan delivery):

1. Deliver more great value. If you are delivering a policy, you are providing the very best value there is to deliver. They should be thrilled with you!
2. Ask a value-seeking question. "We've been through a process to get to this point, have we not? Please tell me the value you feel you've gotten from this process." OR . . ."Tell me what you've learned from this process?"
3. Ask for Introductions!

Can you ask sooner if the timing seems right? Of course! Should you wait with some clients—for them to open up more to the new relationship? Absolutely! But, if you follow this formula as a matter of course, you'll probably be asking more often and in the right away, and best of all, *getting the right Introductions that will help you grow your business.*

Chapter Tumblers—Take-Aways:

 To receive introductions, you have to ask for them.

 You EARN the right to ask by bringing VALUE to the client.

 Are you doing everything to make yourself referrable?

CHAPTER 9

Myths & Truths about Referrals & Introductions

"Ninety percent of this business is beliefs,
and the other half is about activity."

—Don Levin

This business is all about beliefs. It really is psychological. We have to get inside our clients' heads to find their hot button which drives action on their part, but also keep our own heads in the game. That means having the right thoughts and then going beyond thinking about them and implementing an action strategy.

Building your practice on Introductions is not an event, but a life style and a mindset.

You have to constantly be thinking about Introductions, and more importantly, EXPECTING them.

It is about being deliberate and consistent.

It starts with the front talk, and weaving it into the entire tapestry of the home interview, and having the expectation of receiving them. It is just like pulling the application out early to qualify health and leaving it on the table so that it is not a shock but rather anticlimactic at the end of the interview, makes it part of your personal selling process so that it becomes a habit.

It always astounds us that many of the new agents we recruit and train start out very 'gung ho' to ask for introductions but somewhere along the line all seem to fall into the trap of seemingly avoiding them like the plague. We both have spent countless hours talking, training, cajoling and encouraging the harvesting of this low hanging agent generated fruit, and yet, even as we put these thoughts to paper, there are countless agents who can't remember the last time they received, much less asked for, an introduction, even from clients who were probably very receptive to the idea but for the fact that they were never asked!

So why do agents shy away from this wondrous ongoing source of business? We have collected some anecdotes over the years and we'll share some of them now. Hopefully you *won't* see one that you can relate to, but chances are that you will!

- **"I don't give them, so why should I expect them?"**

Ron Willingham, the author of several works to include *Integrity Selling,* refers to this practice of "trading referrals" as psychological reciprocity. By initiating the process with a referral to an advisor, you place him in the position of "owing you one" and thus the relationship is born.

- **"Introductions make it all about me, rather than helping other people."** Positioned correctly, introductions are all about protecting the people that our clients care most about. It is all about them; their families, their friends, business associates. There is absolutely nothing about you in that equation.

- **"Sheer exhaustion. When I am done, I am done, and want to take the money and run."** If you are that exhausted at the end of an interview clearly you talked too much. It is not necessary for you to carry the conversation. In fact, get up and get in front of a mirror right now. You should notice that you have two ears and one mouth. That is the approximate ratio that you should be listening to talking. If the client is doing the talking, you are more apt to be successful. The trick is to listen your way into a sale, not to 'wear them down' with a deluge of facts, figures, and your own stories. In fact, if you know that you are a "Talker", we promise you that if you talk half as much, you will sell twice as much. Take that one to the bank.

- **"The appointment took so long that I didn't want to press my luck."** That sounds like a cross between an excuse and fear. We all know excuses are merely rationalizations to explain our behavior. We'll talk about fear in a short while. Don't fall into this trap.

- **"I forgot."** We call this the Homer Simpson excuse. It's honest and easily correctable—just remember next time and the next time and the next time, until it becomes second nature or a habit to you.

- **"Asking for referrals makes me sound like a salesperson."** The fact is that you *are* a salesperson. People you see *know* that you are a salesperson. They have every expectation that you are going to ask for Introductions. So just do it!

- **Fears:** As we all know, fear is nothing more than False Evidence Appearing Real. It is irrational, and has its roots in many places. So how to deal with it? Let it go.

  o **"I might lose the sale."** At some time, in some place, in a galaxy far far away, we are sure that this happened. It's just that in all the years that we have both been in sales and students of this profession, we have never encountered anyone who has lost a sale simply by *properly* asking for a referral or introduction.

  o **"I might offend the client."** Again, it is a foolish man who takes offense where none was intended. If you are every inch the professional, and conduct yourself as such, it is unlikely that you will offend your client.

o **"I might be perceived as a salesman."** As previously noted above, we *are* sales people. Yes, we are professional in what we do, but deep down in our DNA, we <u>are</u> sales people. Sales can be a noble pursuit if we remain client-centric in all that we say and do in the course of our business pursuits.

o **"What if they say no?"** So what if they do say no. Is it the end of the world or your working relationship with them? Absolutely not. Accept the fact that they are not comfortable with the idea of making an introduction. Don't take it personally—they probably don't mean to offend you! It may be that they have had a bad experience in providing introductions. Make an inquiry about that; and if that is the case, let them know that you are sorry for that, and if they are really not comfortable about providing you with someone to speak with at that time that it is okay. There is always the next meeting!

o **"What if it gets *really* awkward?"** If it gets "awkward" simply because you asked for an introduction, that is an indication of something else being amiss. You may have to employ some fact finding or objection handling tool in order to identify and isolate the real objection behind not providing you with the desired introductions. Again, if it gets "awkward" simply smile, take a step back, and use a non-threatening line such as Bill Cates,' "Don't keep me a secret. I am never too busy to help someone that you care about."

Some other Truths:

• Most people think of Introductions merely as connections to friends and family. Our focus has been on obtaining introductions to their financial professionals; because clients, who will not give you the names of friends and family, are typically more than willing to share the names of other professionals they work with.

It is not what you know or even who you know, but rather who *they* know that matters. The beauty behind building your business on introductions is that the supply of people you can see is infinite. Infinite.

- People you meet via an Introduction are more apt to in turn provide you with Introductions.
- Introductions are a natural result of effective selling
- People see us as sales people and expect us to ask for Introductions
- Introductions will set you free from the limitations of leads
- Self-generated business knows no territorial limits or boundaries.
- Introductions minimize phone time.
- Allows you to grow your client base
- More often than not you will earn more in terms of commission
- You will exponentially reach more people—your clients become your marketing agents.
- Introductions will validate a client's buying decision
- Introductions place the client in the role of mentor/advisor to you
- When they give you permission to use their name that Introduction becomes an endorsement.
- Marketing is a lifestyle, not an event

Remember also that there are three levels of Low Hanging Fruit that we deem introductions:

- Personal—friends and family

  o   These are golden
  o   They are very private.
  o   These are the very people they care about the most and should want to make sure they don't suffer a loss without this coverage-pose the question accordingly.

- Professional—financial advisors, CPAs, attorneys

     o   Clients will generally give you these names.
     o   Makes the call a warm call
     o   Gets you past the gatekeeper
     o   Positions you equally with the professional partner "as we now have a mutual client." That's huge!
     o   Friends who have small businesses

- Social / Group—program coordinator

     o   They will readily give you these names.
     o   No threat to them.

Asking for Introductions is a team effort. It is not all your responsibility. Ask your client "how are we going to get this valuable information to the people that you care about? Should we mail it? E-mail it? Smoke signals? Hand deliver it?"

The worst time to ask for introductions is when you've already closed your sales portfolio, the check or credit card authorization is secured, and it can be perceived as insincere, forced, or as an afterthought.

When is the right time to ask for introductions? All the time, but especially when you deliver policies, call your client with anniversary updates, or invite them to appreciation events or bring value to them in some other way. In summary:

- There is no bad time to ask for Introductions if done properly.
- People *expect* us to ask them for Introductions.
- While surely it has happened somewhere, at some time, the odds of being asked for the check back during the home interview solely because you asked for an Introduction are pretty remote.
- Constantly capture the first and last names of people that they reference so that you can follow up with them in the future.
- It is as simple as learning the ABCs: Activity—Belief—Congruence—Discipline—Expectation—Fearless.
- Just Do It!

Chapter Tumblers—Take-Aways:

 Ask for referrals, don't make excuses.

 Behind every 'no' lurks a 'yes' yearning to get out!

Marketing and obtaining referrals is a lifestyle, not an event.

CHAPTER 10

Dealing with Trusted Sources

"Trusted advisors can become great allies if they have
real experience and perception of a long term care event
involving someone with whom they are close."
—Todd Bothwell

As we continue to market ourselves, building our brand,
networking into strategic alliances, as well as prospecting for
professional partnerships, our preference should be to always work
with people ideally derived from a trusted source. However, we all have
to be mindful that our clients will often be making decisions based
on input from their own trusted sources, which can on occasion run
contrary to prevailing schools of thought and the education we are
attempting to instill in them. In this chapter we will address both of
these scenarios.

So who should be considered a trusted source? By our definition, it is any person that you rely on, and have a high degree of confidence that this advice, if followed, will allow you to take action that will be professionally and personally rewarding. From the client's perspective it would be someone they know who presumably has their best interests at heart and is willing to share constructive advice.

In terms of our clients, the trusted source can be a professional person, but could also be a person they presume has excellent judgment or valuable experience in a given area.

Oddly enough, it can also include the person in the family or inner circle of friends and acquaintances that you may not consider to be qualified to weigh in on such important family matters and life choices. The key is to help them find people who do in fact have the proper perception or experience with the problem at hand and that they are not merely shooting from the hip and just using their influence and ego to assist in making a decision they are really not qualified to make. Many times the people influencing our prospective clients have no monetary or emotional stake in the matter or even more significantly no long term care experience to reference. If their advice is wrong, they will go on with their life and claim no foul, remaining blameless, and not suffer any consequences for a quick "no, you don't need that insurance."

Sometimes the advice givers have a stake and just give poor advice like when concerned family members coach parents on not spending the $3,000 a year on an insurance premium, advice which later costs them thousands of dollars in their inheritance because they told the parents not to purchase a policy with a $500,000 pool of money for long term care expenses because they could "save" or retain the $3,000 over 20 years and accumulate the corpus of $60,000. [This is actually less than the cost of one year's care as this book is being written.]

We have found that people that give advice on long term planning can give good advice or bad advice depending on their real life experience, knowledge of the topic at hand, ability to understand that people age and break down mentally or physically over time, and suffer maladies such as arthritis, dementia, heart issues, as well as those things associated with aging.

How many times have you met a couple and discussed their options as to how to pay for and coordinate their care as they age and they tell you they have to consult their son or daughter about the purchase? Then you inquire about what their son or daughter does for a living and the descriptions they share make it apparent to an outsider that these are likely not the most reliable resources available. At this point you are at a loss as to how to search for some logic or inner strength to advise them that maybe their children should probably not be the "go to" on this decision. Perhaps gently offering that their offspring be a "part of the solution, not the solution" is the way to bring the client back to reality. This is a major decision and if not handled properly will sneak up on couples and families and steal their time, money, and quality of life for years.

People are people, and try as we may, we are not going to change them or who they trust as the trusted adviser. Sometimes they go to friends or neighbors for the "go to" decision, even though you are one of the most knowledgeable people walking the earth with perception, experience, and complete information on all of their options for this type of planning they could ever seek out.

We have had people tell us that "we need to meet with our financial planner first before we make a decision." We then inquire as to whether their planner specializes in asset preservation or income preservation or presents options for long term care planning, or how to select different types of care, all the while knowing the answer we are going to receive from them.

We inquire further: did your planner recommend that you purchase this coverage or did we prompt you to think about the hard fact that you will most likely need care someday? Sometimes the planners recommend it and are advocates for long term care and it would be great for you to find this believer and work with them on designing more long term care plans, and sometimes they become the speed bump in the road and sometimes successfully thwart our attempts to assist these clients in procuring the protection that we know that they so desperately need.

Sometimes these so called 'experts' on whom our clients are relying, quickly dismiss the idea of a long term care plan, and say something like, "you don't need a policy; you have me managing your assets, and so you are good to go."

As we continue to educate the public generally and our clients specifically, when we encounter clients who are receiving 'counter LTCI' advice from their advisors, we always encourage the client to *obtain this advice in writing*, and then inform them that doing so will often allow a sharp attorney to turn this 'advice' into a long term care policy by utilizing a negligence lawsuit against the advisor and his malpractice carrier. That usually sobers up the client and will give them pause to reflect on whether their trusted advisor is as trustworthy as originally thought.

It is interesting to note how times have changed over the past two decades.

Fifteen to twenty years ago many CPAs, attorneys, and financial planners were, as a rule, telling their clients to spend down their assets for long term care cost and not transfer the risk to an insurance company. Now, however, because of changes in the law, legislation enacted by the United States Congress and the various states, as well as rising costs, and longer life expectancies brought on by advances in medicine, any advisor worth his or her salt is recommending some form of long term care planning as part of an overall greater strategy. The reason we know this is because that's what they told *us* most of the time in the 1990's when we tried to partner with them back then . . ."Let the client self-insure this critical need."

What has prompted this change in paradigms across so many professions? We suspect that their perception may have changed when *they* started moving either their own parents or in-laws into their own homes where their spouse will usually become the caregiver by default. Remember that like the rest of us, every trusted adviser usually has four parents to worry about when planning for long term care planning events. They may have already gone through the frustration and turmoil that accompanies this tragic last stage of life that the vast majority of us will encounter if we do not have an exit strategy in place. They may remember when they went through all or spent the lion's share of both parents lifelong hard earned savings and spent hours upon hours searching to get them various types of care provided over the years.

As noted earlier, we are always seeking to associate ourselves with those trusted sources or trusted advisers from whom clients will take advice to protect multiple generations from the costs and hardships that accompany the caring for of spouses or family members. When you find an advocate, especially a professional who has perception and experience about needing a plan for future care you have found an ally to help tell the world about a better way to live and do business for the family.

We would be remiss if we did not talk about those trusted advisers that have huge egos and give reckless or unaccountable sometimes misguided advice. Actually we have been surprised at the number of them practicing out in the public domain. Sometimes clients can trust them too much as evidenced and magnified by people who trusted Bernie Madoff and the like. So just because others admire them for their profession, make sure they keep their ego's in check, make sure they have perception of the magnitude of the problem, that they understand the potential consequences for the poor advice they give people in this area, and help make the best decision for that family. Remember, just because they are respected in their field, it may not be a good idea to have them weigh in on this matter.

Many times they can't control their egos and they want to be the final answer in a family's planning right or wrong and they are not qualified to make that decision. Keep in mind that when these so-called "trusted advisors" retire, they will not take responsibility for the client's care or asset/income depletion.

Please have patience with many of the younger professionals as they do not have the experience and do not realize the potential damage they are doing telling people not to get a plan and transfer the risk. If their parents and grandparents are healthy they have no experience in LTC matters and think no one in their family has ever needed it so no one else needs it either. They could be in positions of managing assets, wills and trusts, bank officers and other positions of authority, own a property and casualty agency, and are clearly not the right person to make the final call, just as we are in no position to pass judgment on their particular field of expertise. There is no instant replay or official review in the Game of Life. The inability to fast forward life twenty years and to view clients with debilitating diseases is an incredible limitation that needs to be addressed.

On the other hand, this book is to give you both sides of the story to help you prepare for the situations you will be encountering and to help you understand that there are some good trusted advisers out there in many financial professional capacities, where you will be extremely happy to work side by side and increase your planning appointments. Helping more people each day, each week, each month, and each year will increase your odds of leading a life of significance.

Chapter Tumblers—Take-Aways:

 "Not all trusted advisors are created equal."

 Not all advisors are qualified and/or have the experience to make these often life-altering decisions that impact multiple generations of a family.

 Tactfully educate your clients about misplaced trust in a tactful manner.

III

The Joint Venture

"The question isn't who is going to let me;
it's who is going to stop me."
—Ayn Rand

CHAPTER 11

Getting Past the Gatekeeper

"Twenty years from now you will be more disappointed by the
things that you didn't do than the ones that you did do."
—Mark Twain

So, you have conducted a home interview and successfully
educated the clients and helped them make an informed decision to
purchase traditional or non-traditional long term care insurance. You
may have even sold them some life insurance or an annuity with which
to pay for the long term care policy, and despite the fact that they
reaped great value from your time together, they were still reticent to
provide any personal introductions to either family or friends. The
good news is that they did give you the name and telephone number
of both their financial advisor and estate planning attorney. So what

do you do with those *professional* referrals that everyone will most assuredly provide you?

When you pick up the phone and dial the number on the business card that your client has thoughtfully provided you, as well as permission to use their name, a live person answers the phone and you very quickly grasp that it is an administrative assistant, secretary, office manager or in other words, the gatekeeper!

So how does one get past the gatekeeper? It's easy. In your most professional and casual voice you are going to say (insert your name) for John Smith please." When she immediately reacts with his/her trained instincts and further queries "What is this in regard to?" you are going to quietly and firmly say, "Mike and Mary Client." More often than not, her reply will be a very subdued, if not cordial, "one moment please."

This should then be followed by another voice coming on the line, namely that of the planner/attorney/advisor, John Smith. The next move is yours and is truly a lot of fun, and goes something like this: "Hi John, (insert your name) here. I am a long term care planning specialist with XYZ Insurance and I had the pleasure of meeting with Mike and Mary Client last evening, and boy do they think the world of you! I mentioned that I have the need of a financial advisor in this area because I sometimes have clients who will ask me for a referral, and when Mike and Mary heard this, they made me promise that I would call you today!"

Naturally the professional on the other end of the line is flattered, and even if he has been approached by other insurance producers, you have been referred by a valued client of his and he has to give you the time of day.

"So John, before I waste your time, or mine, are you accepting new clients?" This will naturally relax him just as warm up is designed to do in the home interview with the client. Now, unless he is at the end of his career and has no desire to implement a succession plan, he will undoubtedly be more than receptive to the idea of additional clients. Please note that we are NOT promising anything at this point, and merely making a natural inquiry as to whether he would entertain additional clients.

Just as we don't sell to the client on the phone, we also don't "sell" to the advisor on the phone. The purpose of this call, as with any lead, is purely to obtain a firm qualified appointment with a partner that is qualified and eager to see us.

"John, because of Mike and Mary's recommendation of you, as well as your interest in taking on additional clientele, I would very much like to meet with you to find out just exactly the type of client you are looking for demographically, as well as whether it would be a good fit for you and me to work together. Quite frankly, I have clients and other professionals provide me with introductions all of the time, and sometimes it takes me back to the nightmares of blind dating. I am going to be in your area both Tuesday and Wednesday of next week, are mornings or afternoons generally better for you?" Sound familiar? The old either/or close designed to keep them choosing between Option A and Option B, resulting in the desired response: an appointment. This appointment can be in the office, for a breakfast or lunch, a cup of coffee, or a drink at the end of the day. That is entirely up to you.

We don't want to get into a protracted discussion on the phone, but merely to set an appointment. After that you are going to do your due diligence, check out any potential websites that he may be operating, membership in any professional organizations, as well simply employing social services such as Google, LinkedIn, and Facebook.

If you feel comfortable with the way the call is going you may want to ask an additional question before getting off the phone, such as "do you recommend long term care insurance to your clients?" This is particularly appropriate (and safe to do) if Mike and Mary have clued you in that he does bring it up in the course of his regular advisory consultations.

That is how you get past the gatekeeper. If you do not have a client's name to utilize, you can usually get passed the gatekeeper by saying that you were referred to the advisor or that "John has come to our attention as someone we may be in a position to refer clients to, assuming that John is accepting clients. Is he available to chat a moment?"

The key is to pick up the phone and to utilize all of your centers of influence in an effort to grow your network of professionals to whom you can make referrals and even better, receive them back. This takes us back to Ron Willingham's Law of Psychological Reciprocity. By initiating the process with a referral to an advisor, you place him in the position of "owing you one" and thus the relationship is born. In the absence of a contractual business arrangement, a a best practice to be followed would be to implement a one for one exchange of referrals program to prevent the relationship from becoming too one-sided which can cause resentment to build and cripple the relationship.

Again, we are not merely looking for access to his book of business, but rather, are offering him a time-tested, completely effective turn-key marketing system by which he can offer to his clients the protection of long term care insurance and more importantly your professional services in this critical decision making process.

Chapter Tumblers—Take-Aways:

 Getting past the gatekeeper requires the use of a process albeit a simple one.

 It all starts by asking our clients and COIs "how's that working out for you."

 Nothing happens unless you pick up the phone.

CHAPTER 12

Identifying the Decision-maker

"We offer a turnkey business model to professionals
with marketing, sales competency, and compliance,
and not just another referral program."
—Todd Bothwell

Quite often, the introduction you receive may be to an advisor or professional who is part of a larger firm. Even though he acts "independently", there may be firm requirements or restrictions on outside business activities (OBA) that he may not be allowed to engage in with outside vendors, either because of contractual or firm or broker-dealer restrictions. For this reason, your first task is to determine who the actual decision maker within the entity is, and assuming that the relationship will go forward, whether an individual or the firm will be receiving compensation.

You will save endless hours of frustration if you know who the decision maker is and avoid those who merely act as if they are the decision maker, but ultimately lack the requisite authority to enter into an agreement with you.

Unfortunately, some of your challenge may entail having to navigate through each firm's chain of egos. On occasion you will find yourself being treated like a hot potato and being shuttled between otherwise disinterested employees who may or may not have the owners interest at heart, while on other occasions you may find yourself being introduced to the "product specialist" for the firm or sometimes if all goes according to plan, and ultimately the best case scenario, the owner.

The question to ask, and ideally identify upfront while conducting your pre-interview research, is:

Who is ultimately responsible for the addition of financial services for the firm's clients? If you know this going into the firm's business office, you may be able to avoid being sent to the person in charge of getting rid of salespeople; the numbers oriented accountant; the top financial planner, the compliance officer, the marketing employee, and ideally find yourself in front of the owner.

Remember, we are not merely proposing another referral program or seeking access to their book of business for our own benefit but rather are offering their firm a turnkey marketing system by which they can bring this added level of protection to their clientele and through which they can safeguard their clients' financial health and future as well as their own.

The owner of the business has much to gain by working with you, and conversely a great deal to lose if they opt not to work with you. As with our clients, it is all about education. You need to be able to articulate the particulars associated with both scenarios.

The gains are numerous:

- Retention of the clients they have worked so hard to obtain by adding both a valuable service and product;
- Preservation of funds under management;
- Increased revenue flow for the firm; for example, one sale per week could be in excess of $50,000 of additional annual revenue.

- Keep out competitors who would sell long term care insurance to their client and conceivably attempt to pull away the money management, annuity, or life business. To this end, you may have to allay the fear that we will solicit sales for any products other than the one we were brought in to handle. This can be done as simply as with an e-mail from you to the producer.

- You become another asset of the firm—literally a six-figure marketing specialist at no cost to them. We would encourage you to offer the opportunity for them to add you to their website as the product specialist. This is yet another enhancement for the firm that costs neither one of you any additional working capital.

- The owner realizes his firm has you as the new product specialist to market their services (these might include wills and trusts if an attorney or assets under management, if an advisor) to additional new clients.

Example: Client "A" is referred to you and you design and implement a long term care insurance policy. Client "A" is pleased with your service, professionalism, and finds so much value in your meeting that she then tells her sister and brother to buy long term care insurance from you as well. As a result of these introductions, you now have the opportunity to send two new clients back to the financial planner or professional business partner.

Six primary concerns that you must remember at all times when dealing with the owner or ultimate decision-maker:

1. He/she is likely afraid you will risk or jeopardize the relationship with their client and lose the client.
2. He/she wants you to help them grow their core business
3. He/she does not want to lose their core business focus
4. They do not want to add a lot of expense/overhead
5. They want to be in compliance with everything they do
6. Additional income through commission splits is usually last on the list so don't be too quick to dangle a rich contract in front of him unless it is clear that an alternate or replacement income stream is of paramount importance to him.

The business owner may also be looking for ways to differentiate the firm from like professionals or, again, may be looking to you to replace diminished commissions or lost revenue channels.

Some firms have multiple business partners and owners and you need to know how they manage the day to day decision making.

Sometimes we get excited when we sign a firm on to do business with us and think the firm is going to really be good for us and, nothing happens. Nothing *will* happen at the beginning or throughout the relationship unless the decision maker makes it clear that the employees are expected to set up a number of appointments each month for you with clients that may need Long Term Care Insurance.

Todd found while working with over one hundred CPA and Law firms in a previous career that if the managing partner did not "enforce and endorse" long term care planning for their clients and enforce by telling his employee's that they were expected to introduce clients to our specialist the referrals never happened. The most successful firms would place referring clients in the employee's job description and measure how many referrals the employee gave for their employee review. They could exceed expectations, meet expectations, or fall below set expectations.

If you are committed to working with advisors in firms, this top down approach is necessary to have a successful business relationship. The owner must lead with a policy of leadership attitude of endorse [the new planning specialist] and enforce [that everyone will work diligently to refer clients to you.] He or she can do this by literally walking up and down the hall, poking his/her head into offices and cubicles and asking "how many appointments have you set this week for Todd to visit with your clients to discuss long term care?" If this does not happen, you will likely be relegated to a back burner and quickly forgotten.

Chapter Tumblers—Take-Aways:

 It is absolutely critical to find the decisionmaker early on.

 Be mindful of their concerns and the value you bring to them!

The Partners need to 'endorse and enforce' LTC planning in their firm!

CHAPTER 13

The First Meeting

"Always be prepared to listen to the professional partner's story;
there are always reasons that their name is on the marquis."
—Todd Bothwell

As previously noted, prior to your first meeting with any professional partner, it is imperative that you learn as much as possible about the individual that started the firm and whether that person is the same person that now runs the successful enterprise.

With this information in hand, you are now prepared for the first meeting with your potential new partner. Just as with the home interview, we want to get that person talking to us by asking open ended questions after conducting necessary warm up.

After we talk about the demographics of their typical client, we want to do an even deeper dive with them and their practice so as to ascertain the degree of success associated with this partnership. Some questions to help you get started are listed below:

- When was the business started?
- Why was the business started?
- Was the initial capital for the business acquired or was it built on sweat equity?
- What differentiates this business from the competition?
- What prompted him/her to own his/her business?
- What will their company look like in five years if all goes as planned?
- If five years from now they look back to gauge their success what transpired in order for them to have achieved this success?
- Out of all the people in the community why is their name on the door or sign of the company?

You need to get a sense of their value system and what they admire. Once you get a feel for how the operation is run and what makes it thrive, you can start positioning your service to help them retain clients and grow their core business. Learn as much about them as possible on the first visit. Determine whether you can envision yourself working closely and for long hours with this individual. If not, don't! Do you initially trust or have a good feeling about this person or firm? Remember, you are not desperate and that there are many other professional partner offices that *would* love to offer senior services that include LTC planning solutions and Medicare/Medicaid issues and welcome your assistance in doing so with their clients.

Some questions you need to ask about the clients and households serviced:

- Do they have the health and wealth for your products?
- Do they have discretionary income not only for the initial purchase, but subsequent purchases?
- How many families/households does the professional serve? (Not how many tax returns do they complete if CPA's, but rather how many families.) Many firms will complete multiple tax returns for the same client(s) or attorneys may create

several entities for one family. One family may complete and file as many as ten returns, but it is still one family or household to you.

Other questions to ask the owner on the first visit:

- Has the owner ever known anyone who has needed any type of care?
- Does the owner own a LTC policy? Why or Why not?
- Is it important to them that their clients work with a highly skilled and trained LTC specialist?
- Is it important to them to maintain the appearance of independence and objectivity in working with a long term care agent? (Multiple companies are usually preferred rather than the appearance they are working for a captive one company agent).
- Does he have goals similar to ours for their clients? (Wanting them to have quality care later in life, have a written plan and transfer the financial risk to an insurance company, to maintain their independence and control; avoid government programs like Medicaid, have professional assistance in planning and managing care and to have the peace of mind that comes with a plan.)
- (We will discuss commission sharing in a later chapter)
- Does he understand and want additional residual income coming in when he retires?
- Does he realize this income, called insurance renewals, will either increase the value of the firm or he can exclude the insurance renewals from the eventual sale of their business and keep it for part of his retirement income?
- Does the owner perceive any liability if he/she does not offer LTC planning to their clients from the clients or their family circle?
- Will the owner reinforce and help us manage the process with the firm's employees? (Our previously discussed policy of Endorse and Enforce)
- How many employees does he have and does he have a marketing department?

- Do they perform client reviews now? If so, have him explain the process to you.

Remember you want to integrate your service into his and not disrupt their core business. If there is sufficient reason to believe that this is potentially a strong match, and that a working relationship can be established, set up the second meeting.

Chapter Tumblers—Take-Aways:

 The First Meeting is critical and is all about them, and not you.

 The focus has to remain on building their primary business and not selling LTCI.

 You are of great value to them—is your proposed partner of equal worth to you?

CHAPTER 14

Second Meeting: Ground Rules

"The partner must jump in and earn their 50%; you
can't will it to be done . . . He needs to pull his weight
by driving the business within the firm."
—Todd Bothwell

The second meeting is all about establishing the ground rules
of the relationship, and determining who will take on what portion
of the work load. This is a key element in determining whether this
relationship is going to flourish or wither on the vine.

Once you find yourself in the second meeting with your interested
professional partner prospect you need to discuss how the process
will work in terms of marketing to their clients; setting the client
appointments, conducting the appointments, communication to the

firm about their clients on a weekly basis, and the tracking system used to follow the applications to policy issue.

As a result, the following are the key questions that must be addressed in the course of the second interview:

- How is the business owner going to let the clients know about this new service?

We will discuss marketing in another chapter and the most effective manner in which to get clients out of the file cabinet or computer data base and to a home or office interview.

- Who will be the Champion at the firm that will be responsible for the ultimate success or failure of their new senior services venture?
- Who will be available and accountable to us during the initial launch and for an ongoing basis after launch? Most firms will appoint one person to be the driver of the new business and that person would hold the other people/employees in the firm accountable.

In some firms, it is solely the owner who contacts clients and meets with them to review their accounts and financial plans, while in other firms there may be an accounts manager or assistant who maintains this relationship and will actually be the person in contact with the clients and arranging the interviews. In other firms, communications may be in the form of newsletters, updates, e-mail, or conventional letter that serves as an invitation to the client to come in for an appointment.

Because you are going to become an integral part of the advisor's professional staff, it is imperative that the professional partner has a person designated to manage the calendar of the long term care agent's availability each week or month especially in those cases where there are multiple advisors in the same office all of whom may be looking to book appointments with only one agent. To accomplish this, we recommend some form of calendar sharing program where administrative people can view the one shared calendar and book appointments.

While the use of a shared calendar software may sound like an overly obvious thing to mention, we have found that, "the devil is in the details", and this is one aspect of the relationship that you always want to go smoothly so as no not become a source of embarrassment for either one of you in the event that multiple appointments are scheduled in conflict with one another.

In addition to scheduling actual [selling] appointments, it is also important to establish ground rules regarding what is going to be a governing and acceptable response time to one another. Often there will be issues which require joint decisions that will enable the partnership to move forward and to flourish. Both parties need to be comfortable with the parameters that are selected. The parties need to be mutually respectful and return one another's emails and phone calls within 24 hours to keep the service at a level geared to serving the client most efficiently.

In the event that you plan to deliver a series of seminars, workshops, or client appreciation/referral events, it is especially important to establish firm ground rules and to delineate responsibilities for all of the actions necessary for these events to be properly planned and executed. We cannot stress enough the importance attached to the use of a comprehensive checklist which identifies all tasks and the person who will bear the responsibility for each task. These tasks may include:

- Who is going to bear the costs associated with the activity
- The coordination that usually will begin approximately twelve weeks out for each activity
- Site selection
- The program or activity content
- Materials to be utilized
- Compliance approval for materials to include invitations
- The ancillary follow up with all attendee's and materials that will be utilized.

Other issues to be addressed and identified:

- Who will call the clients and introduce the new service?
- Who has the best relationship with the client at that firm?

- Identifying when invitations will be made. Most owners have close contact with between 50 and 100 clients, which is a nice start, but certainly is only the tip of the iceberg in firms with 1000 clients or more. What happens to the other 900 clients the owner knows, but does not have that strong of a relationship?
- Accordingly, how many customers does this firm have to contact that have health; income; and assets suitable for a LTC preservation product?

As we venture deeper into larger firms with multiple advisors, and often multiple levels of advisors, it is imperative that everyone shares the same mutual expectations and level of commitment. In the event that this does not occur, you may find yourself bitterly disappointed. For example, if each of six partners at the firm has one thousand clients, you would logically assume that you would have access to six thousand clients. In reality, you will only have access to each partner's clients if that partner has bought in to our business model. What you may experience is that one or two partners of a multi partner firm will join your cause. If they have success and it doesn't cost the other partners a loss of clients or provides them with an increased revenue stream without an ancillary time drain, they may join you as well later. They will send the partners over the hill first and if they do not have arrows in them when they return you may have a shot at working with them.

The servicing planner or LTC agent needs to keep the owner and other participants supplied with current information each week on their clientele. This failure to communicate is why most relationships do not successfully launch or survive past the first couple of client referrals. If we take a moment and place ourselves in the shoes of the professional partner, we see that he is agreeing to enter into a partnership with another professional who is going to be a total reflection on him. We are asking him to trust a third party to work with his clients. We must be respectful of them, as they must be respectful of our clients that we refer to them, as we mutually build a larger client base. We must control the delivery of information through answering questions or researching answers for the clients. If and when clients call the partner to discuss the planning you have done for them;

make sure the partner is apprised of what is going on with that case or he/she may be cast in a poor light that is not going to benefit either one of you. If the partner is ever in the position where he has to tell the client "I do not know, I need to call my specialist," not only is that an extra step, but it also create stress which may lead the partner to determine that the relationship is not to his liking. He will soon feel it to be a burden that he will rid himself of by stopping the referral process, and usually the agent never knows what went wrong.

The second appointment should also be used to manage expectations and establish a timeline that all agree to honor. The timeline should consist of milestones and dates of completion which will be checked off before launch. Items to be addressed include:

- Any potential insurance State licensing
- Any state mandated LTCI partnership courses
- Appointment process from the insurance company
- The length of time the firm will require to profile their data base with clients to call about our new service
- The length of time to have any requisite Compliance issues such as materials that are to be utilized with the marketing portion of the program

At the same time, unless you are subject to an umbrella contract that binds both you and the partner, you should also address what the profit sharing for you and the firm and the firms planners looks like, who will be the lead champion at the firm to drive the success of the new program, how many partners are going to be involved, and other important elements the firms need to make the other partner firm work with their existing dynamics. The financial aspect of the relationship and what a potential split looks like will be addressed in a later chapter.

Marketing to professionals is incredibly rewarding and is a great way to exponentially expand the scope of your individual business and allow you to leverage yourself in ways you may not have previously considered. While it is rewarding, and the pros far outweigh the cons, be mindful of the fact that most professionals are very territorial and fear that you may directly or indirectly compromise the relationship that they enjoy with their clients. Therefore it is imperative that you establish, upfront, the scope of your relationship, e.g. you will only talk to the client about Long Term Care or a hybrid life insurance product that contains a long term care rider, and be subject to a non-compete as it applies to all other products. Other challenges include having to manage around the various egos you will encounter, as well the need to make everyone feel good about going into business with us. You will be engaged in a solid relationship if the decision makers don't need to be right all the time and, more importantly, if they have the ability to listen and learn about new ways to succeed that we have already proven in our field as we have served our own clients.

You want to integrate a system for each firm so it works for them. Do not plan on each firm doing things the same way. While a good bit of what we are addressing is easily replicable, the nature of relationships will dictate the manner in which you may have to modify your agreement. The good news is we can be versatile and integrate into most firms in the country and help as many clients in the senior planning areas of asset preservation, income preservation, as well as providing independence, control, and quality healthcare later in life.

Chapter Tumblers—Take-Aways:

 Each firm has its own identity and culture. Never forget this fact.

 This is a business process—know it and respect it.

 Life and Business is all about commitments. Both parties have to honor them.

CHAPTER 15

The Dance Begins

"We can do it the easy way or the hard way. We always have that choice. Marketing to Professionals is definitely the easy way."
—Don Levin

Marketing to Professionals on behalf of our agents has been a personally rewarding experience for us over the years as both agents and as sales leaders. As graduates of the School of Hard Knocks we *know* that these relationships either flourish or wither on the vine dependent upon mutual expectations and commitment among partners, and the presence of both a business plan and a marketing plan.

Since you have already been through the home interview equivalent of Warm Up while initially setting this appointment or being introduced to one another; it is now time to move to the Need section of the interview and obtain answers to the following questions:

"John, why am I here today? What is the main reason that you want to introduce long term care insurance to your clients?" After asking these questions, sit back, close your mouth and open your ears. Take notes as you would with a client interview and let the professional provide you with the "why" or the purpose of your partnership. It may be their desire to protect their clients' assets, to safeguard their own professional income strategies, or to shelter themselves from the ancillary liability of being in a fiduciary relationship with their client. The reasons will vary. The importance of this step is ascertaining their motivation by slowly peeling the onion.

We also want to know if the advisor has had any personal experience with long term care in either his family or with any of his existing clients. We both have found that where this experience is present, the advisor will be a true believer and in turn possess the *urgency* to bring this vital protection to his clientele. If he has dealt with this in his immediate family we want to personalize it by having him bring the past to the present by relating his role in this experience:

- How did he feel when confronted with this issue?
- Who was the person who required caregiving?
- Who provided this caregiving?
- How long did it go on?
- Who bore the burden of the expense?
- Was he personally involved in the caregiving?
- How did it impact his life?
- What was his role?
- Where did it take place?

In any event, we want to bring him back to the event much in the same manner that we do with a client!

If he has experienced this caregiving with *a client*, we want to know:

- What it was like for the family and for the client?
- What role did he serve in the process? How did this make *him* feel?

- What impact did it have on his practice or firm?
- What was the ultimate financial outcome?

Of paramount importance is the question of whether he has his own long term care policy. If he does, why? If not, why not? Just as with the client, we need to know the level of commitment this person has to our product, the degree of need he associates with it, and the level of urgency he will convey to those who will hopefully become your mutual clients.

We both like to accompany agents to these meetings, because as the "outsider" to the budding relationship we can often say and do things that the agent cannot do for himself.

To this end, we will often dictate where everyone sits just as we take charge in the Home Interview with clients. Why is where people sit important? Because our objective when accompanying an agent to these preliminary meetings is to help forge not only a working relationship but a true partnership of equals. For this reason if we are sitting in a restaurant or coffee house, I will endeavor to have them sit together on the same side of the booth or to position their chairs at the table so that they are sitting near one another and I am across from *them*. I never want it to appear that it is a two on one in our favor, but rather that *they* are the team and I am the odd man out. We never want our agent to feel subordinate to the financial professional but rather an equal in terms of professional acumen and technical ability. Our greatest commodity is, in fact, our expertise and advice which is why we should all be thinking in terms of offering solutions and not product.

We will then say to the advisor, "John, the relationship that you are contemplating with Jane will either flourish or wither on the vine dependent upon two things: mutual expectations and commitment. The mutual expectations can be defined in terms of a business plan which may be as simple as' how many clients do you want to help each year' or 'how much money do you want to make' and a marketing plan which will define the 'how to' associated with getting Jane in front of your clients so that she can be the point of sale subject matter expert in regard to long term care insurance products. We'll talk about these two plans shortly." We'll actually address the Business Plan in Chapter 21 and the Marketing Plan in Chapters 22 and 23.

We will then continue to wear the "black hat" so that the agent can continue to wear the "white hat," and carry the water by addressing commitment so that the advisor is fully aware of the level of the agent's commitment to making this relationship a successful one and to take another barometer reading in terms of the advisor's own commitment.

"Before we talk about these plans however, we believe that it would be appropriate to talk about the commitment requisite to making this relationship a success. Allow me to illustrate how we define commitment by sharing a story with you" . . .

Farmer Brown had a wonderful farm on which he grew a number of different crops and had a great many animals. He and his family were largely self-sufficient and took pride in the fact that they could feed themselves with a well-rounded diet. The Browns took good care of their livestock, and in some cases they were as much a part of the family as were the family dogs and cats.

One day, out in the barnyard, the Cow, the Chicken and the Pig were having a conversation about their commitment to the Brown family.

"You know, I really like the Browns. As people go, they are okay in my book. That is why I provide them with Grade A quality eggs for the breakfast table 365 days a year. Nothing is too good for the Browns," said the Chicken.

"Oh yeah? You call laying some eggs *commitment*? That's easy stuff! Where do you think the milk, the butter, and the cheese that they eat every day comes from, hmm," asked the Cow.

The pig in the meantime was being reflective as he listened to this exchange, and after scratching his chin with his hoof, said, "I gotta tell you both, you *both* have it pretty easy. Eggs, milk, cheese, butter. Big deal. You want *real* commitment? Me and the other boys are providing the bacon for breakfast and the ham for Sunday Supper! That ladies, is real commitment."

At this point, I will look the advisor in the eye and state, "Jane is committed to this relationship. I have seen her deliver to other partners over the years in a very consistent and professional manner.

"So John, how would you categorize yourself in terms of commitment to this relationship and in offering long term to your clients? Are you the chicken, the cow, or the pig? How committed are you to this new partnership? Jane is going to do everything humanly possible to be another professional member of your team that will always place the interests of your client ahead of everything else, and to be a natural complement to you, and to make you look good to your clients."

Some might think this a juvenile approach, but historically great lessons have been taught in parables, and this is a modern day parable that I have used for many years with a great deal of success.

Once you know that the professional is committed to the concept of long term care insurance, then we can proceed to develop the business and marketing plans which will provide the framework of the partnership and establish milestones, the adherence to which will insure success of the venture, but most importantly provide a new generation of clients with the protection they so sorely need Today in order to safeguard their Tomorrows.

> "Every great dream begins with a dreamer. Always remember, you have within you the strength, the patience, and the passion to reach for the stars to change the world."
> —Harriet Tubman.

Chapter Tumblers—Take-Aways:

 Commitment is everything; without it we have nothing more than an illusion.

 As with our clients, partners who have been 'touched' by these [LTC] experiences make better partners.

 It's a numbers game; just as with selling, not every prospective partner appointment is going to be a match. It all boils down to Need, Urgency, and Value.

CHAPTER 16

How to go Out of Business in a Hurry

"People who succeed have momentum. The more they succeed,
the more they want to succeed, and the more they find a way to
succeed. Similarly, when someone is failing, the tendency is to get on
a downward spiral that can even become a self-fulfilling prophecy."
—Tony Robbins.

We have both learned over the years that relationships with professional partners are no different than the personal intimate relationships that we enjoy with spouses/partners, family members, and close friends. They all require our attention and loving care, because in the absence of such things, the relationship can come apart far faster than it went together. In this chapter we will be discussing several ways your professional partner relationship can go south, most notably in the beginning of the relationship and less so during the relationship.

We will also recount the most dangerous things that can end a great run. Most of this will not be a surprise to you.

In the early stages of the relationship you need to over communicate with each other; don't be afraid to remind one another, by agreement, as to what each of you mutually agreed to do under the terms of your partnership agreement. It is your mutual responsibility, though in reality most of it will fall on to your shoulders, to make sure each partner moves the relationship forward by doing what they initially promised to do. Most relationships wither because one, or both, partners get busy and do not make the partner relationship and associated duties a high priority. You need to set mutual deadlines that are both realistic and comfortable for both of you. For example, set a realistic timeline milestone date by which you will provide the promised client letter that your advisor partner can in turn utilize to contact his clients, while your partner is identifying the first fifty clients that need to be contacted, and called into the office to start the planning process. This process may be a policy review for those clients who may already be policyholders, or newly identified clients who need to have their options explained to them, when measured against the financial risk associated with self-insurance.

The single largest contributor to failed relationships is in fact unmet expectations. These can damage any relationship and leave one party disillusioned or feeling ignored or let down to the point where they will eventually stop trying to make the relationship work.

While you want to be optimistic and upbeat, and build enthusiasm for the relationship, always be honest about what is going to be required of the partner and/or their firm and staff. The more you can give your new partner in full disclosure up front about the licensing requirements, long term care certification, errors and omissions insurance, and the various and sundry potential pitfalls associated with the appointment process, all the better. Surprises never work to your advantage.

The number one reason we have identified that prevents potentially outstanding partners from going into business with you is that they have legitimate fears that you may cause them to lose a quality paying client. It's not a fear that you will steal them, but rather the risk of placing their hard earned clients in front of you and that you may say or do something that may cost them that client. Some advisors will be myopic enough so as to mentally weigh the predictable income made each year from that client against the potential amount of any additional income stream that your skills make provide to them. In most cases it is easy to demonstrate why this risk is minimal in nature and how this irrationally based fear could prevent them from realizing significant income they will make by properly executing your proposed alliance and in providing a new service or product through you to the rest of their clients. That being said, please realize that we acknowledge that this fear of you saying something that may sound too much like a salesperson or that you will be late or not follow through like they do with the client, could cost them a client is not without basis and definitely should be addressed right up front. Failure to do so may be disastrous because this fear can paralyze them into inactivity and prevent them from ever launching with you to reap a large reward. Silly as it sounds, they may be so shortsighted as to be thinking about the single $1,500 tax return fee or other product commission that could be jeopardized as opposed to the potential of gaining $1,000 commissions on their nine hundred other clients or $900,000. Illogical as that sounds to a sales person, professional partners do have this fear and it is legitimate and logical to them. Remember, perception is reality.

If you are wondering why a financial advisor might not want to work with you, consider the following example. A financial advisor or investment adviser who can place a single client's assets of $500,000 under management, and then charge a fee of 1% and garner $5,000 each year does not need to "sell" them anything else. They make that money without any health qualifying or the asking of any invasive health questions. If they perform around the agreed risk parameters and provide fair rates of return each year they continue to get paid the 1% or $5,000 or more as the account grows. By trying to have you offer a long term care policy to preserve assets and income for a client, they need to subject the client to an interview with you; the client will need to have a medical assessment company conduct a paramed exam and possibly a cognitive interview with a nurse. So they may choose the path of least resistance and not have you offer LTC planning to their clients, because if the client has a bad experience with you or the insurance company or the medical services company conducting the examination, they may not only choose not to pursue the insurance product but go so far as to pull their money management account as well, thus *costing* the advisor the coveted $5,000 annual income forever.

They also harbor legitimate fears about their reputations. If they do business with you they, in essence, endorse you and they have to live with your actions professionally and personally as well. This is great if you live a respectable life but can be a disaster for them if your reputation is ever tarnished and they are painted with the same broad brush and in essence can be 'guilty by association' through affiliation with you. Naturally this applies to you and them equally.

You know you are seeing signs of a rocky partnership if the professional partner does not return your calls or emails in a timely manner. If this lack of discipline or respect manifests itself early in the game it lets you know that the new business venture is not what you thought it was and they are not completely buying into the process or giving it the time or priority it needs to get the operation off the ground.

As noted, mutual expectations and commitment are the bedrock of this relationship. Both of you have to work hard for the new venture to work. First and foremost, both parties meeting the agreed upon deadlines is the key to the new business partnerships successfully negotiating the rapids.

A potential partner's ego may be HUGE and make it impossible for them to let another outsider take control of their client even if it is only for a two hour presentation and to complete the paperwork. It might be they love to star in the "Me, Myself & I" show, and find they can't share the client spot light with you. By all means, move on!

In the event your partner is part of a larger organization, and they have employees, do his leadership skills include those of being a good delegator? This allows him to not only endorse you but enforce your service and require that other employees look for customers who need your services. Is it going to be part of their employee review if they don't send clients to you? Are they willing to establish minimum standards that have to be met in order for them to receive a good employee review, thus entitling them to a salary raise as well?

Is he a good business owner and does he understand the leverage you bring to his firm to meet with their clients on this important topic? Do they recognize that you help them retain clients for the firm, that you increase the planning value of the firm in the senior issues area, and that you keep other professionals on the outside that may want to sell the LTC and then later sneak in and take an annuity sale, tax return, other employee benefit sales, or property and casualty business away or any other business they offer their clients.

Finally, does he want to do the right thing for his clients to preserve their assets and income with a plan? Is he willing to humble himself by bringing in an expert—You—to help them assist their clients with a product they need in order to preserve their life style? We certainly hope that he will want to have you join his team of experts and prevent their clients from having to leave themselves at the mercy of product pushers where their clients are sold products from less trained and qualified LTC planners and to fend for themselves with aggressive hungry insurance salespeople.

> "All relationships are about expectations . . .
> both met and unmet."
> —Todd Bothwell.

Chapter Tumblers—Take-Aways:

 Are parternship values in alignment? To be successful this is a must!

 There are a few legitimate reasons that will preclude the formation of a partnership with you. Be aware of them and address them head on in the course of the interview process.

 Fear of loss can be more powerful than the Desire for Gain.

CHAPTER 17

The Pitfalls: Caution Before You Proceed

"Develop success from failures. Discouragement and failure
are two of the surest stepping stones to success."
—Dale Carnegie

It is imperative that you never forget that our business is just that:
a business that serves the general public fraught with many perils to
the consumer and producer alike. As such, it is controlled by State
and Federal regulations that must be adhered to at all times. While
engaged in a strategic alliance or actual contractual partnership, it is
imperative that all parties abide by all applicable laws, regulations, and
company policies.

Quite often, the individual financial advisor or advisory firm will
be bound by Compliance rules and regulations promulgated by their
organization, their Broker-Dealer, and/or by FINRA. To this end, it is

imperative that you never place yourself or your partner in jeopardy of violating any of these rules.

More often than not, when agents find themselves in a precarious position, it is the result of ignorance or haste, or worse, a blatant disregard for the rules or rationalization. "It's just an invitation. Why does it have to go to Compliance?" Yes, even something as simple as a dinner invitation being sent to clients will often require approval from the Compliance Department. Don't forget to check in with Compliance on regular basis. While some will refer to Compliance as the "Don't Patrol" or "Sales Prevention Department" our experience has been that a cooperative relationship with these professionals is a great way to prolong your career, avoid fines, penalties and costly delays, and to reap the bounty that you are seeking through this cooperative venture. Take the time to do it right.

Keep in mind as well that regardless of the actual relationship established between the parties, when applications are submitted with both partners named as cooperating agents that you are inextricably bound to one another and can be held liable for the acts of commission or omission of the other. For this reason it is imperative that you both have the proper levels of Errors and Omissions (E&O) insurance required by your carrier and regulating agencies.

On the non-legal side of things, it is also critical that you establish from the beginning what role each of you will play in the partnership with clearly defined roles and responsibilities to include how the costs associated with events, mailings, and promotions will be divided. We will talk about the manner in which production credit may be shared in chapter 21.

If both parties are committed to the success of the venture, a solid system of regular communication is established, and expectations are realistic, this will be a successful partnership.

Chapter Tumblers—Take-Aways:

 There are no short cuts involving Compliance.

 Your competition is waiting for the opportunity to sink you if you do cut corners.

 Build your business on the solid foundation of Compliance so that you don't lose your business and renewals!

CHAPTER 18

Laws Never to be Broken

"It is our choices, that show what we truly
are, far more than our abilities."
—J.K. Rowling

Why should we be talking about laws and regulations when we said that we were going to focus on marketing and networking and developing strategic alliances? It is because as licensed insurance producers and financial advisors, we are offering health insurance products to the general public, and all parties doing so are bound by laws such as the Health Insurance Portability and Accountability Act of 1996 (HIPAA) which was enacted by the United States Congress and signed into law by President Bill Clinton in 1996. While we all know it simply as "HIPAA" it is formally known as the Kennedy-Kassebaum Act.

Title I of HIPAA, which largely does not impact us, essentially protects health insurance coverage for workers and their families when they change or lose their jobs.

Title II of HIPAA, ironically known as the Administrative Simplification (AS) provisions (ironic because there is absolutely nothing simple about it administratively), requires the establishment of national standards for electronic transactions and national identifiers for providers, health insurance plans, and employers. As licensed producers, we are definitely included under these provisions.

Title II specifically defines policies, procedures and guidelines for maintaining the privacy and security of individually identifiable health information as well as outlining numerous offenses relating to health care and sets civil and criminal penalties for violations. This is the scary and very expensive aspect of our work that everyone has to pay close attention to because failure to do so can be catastrophic. Depending on just how you err, your E&O carrier may be reticent to either defend you or indemnify your actions.

Title II also requires the Department of Health and Human Services (HHS) to draft rules aimed at increasing the efficiency of the health care system by creating standards for the use and dissemination of health care information. This is where the infamous HIPAA form comes into play. While we are uncertain that the drafters of this legislation ever envisioned multiple versions of the same form being utilized in various branch offices of the same medical facility or doctor's office, ours is not to reason why, but simply to comply. The single largest time aspect of our underwriting process usually centers on our ability to obtain medical records from our clients' health care providers. Don't fight it, just go along with it, and involve your clients. A call from them to the doctor's office is usually far more effective than a call from either you or the company's vendor.

What you absolutely must never forget is that as licensed producers we have a duty to safeguard and prevent the disclosure of Protected Health Information (PHI). PHI is defined as any information which concerns health status, provision of health care, or payment for health care that can be linked to an individual. The penalties for each violation associated with such disclosures are pretty hefty, typically running in the thousands of dollars, and will definitely ruin your day.

So how do you avoid these problems? By exercising caution and vigilance with the information that you retain in client files and shredding applications and other non-essential documents as soon as possible after submission of the application. Most companies retain this information for you digitally so there is no reason for you to retain it as well. Back in the day, we were required to obtain social security numbers on applications. This alone made it imperative that these files were secured properly. We suggest merely retaining those interview notes that are helpful in re-creating the conversation that led to the development of the plans and strategies that you ultimately provided to your client(s). Keep them locked up in your office, and if you are utilizing a laptop computer in the course of your business, make sure that you are utilizing appropriate encryption software (usually provided by your company or available commercially) and that you limit access to your computer. This means that screens should not be visible to the public in your office, and if you are sitting in Starbucks or Panera, be very mindful that public Wi-Fi systems are not secure and could be an opportunity for less reputable people to steal this information and create a situation where you could be held liable.

When you get a new computer, insure that you destroy the hard drive in the old computer. If your computer is lost or stolen, it is your responsibility to report the loss to your company's compliance department who will assist you in reporting it to HHS. These are very serious issues so do not leave it sitting unattended in public or in your car.

Something else that we often overlook is the fact that anyone you may utilize as an appointment setter or within the partner's firm who may be asking health questions of the client or have access to this information must be licensed as well.

Along these same lines, remember that no one can grant permission to you to call someone who has their name and telephone number on a Do Not Call Registry. For this reason alone, it is imperative that you always observe the proper rules of "phoning etiquette" and never *assume* that you are "good to go" to make a phone call unless you have received expressed permission to do so.

Follow these basic rules and you can avoid these legal headaches and flourish as a planning specialist.

Chapter Tumblers—Take-Aways:

 Insure that your practice complies with HIPAA.

 Ignorance and denial of the law is never a good defense.

 The safeguarding of client information is serious business and must be reflected in all of our business practices.

IV

MARKETING MECHANICS

"Don't let the fear of losing be greater than
the excitement of winning."
—Robert Kiyosaki

CHAPTER 19

Big Firms v. Independents

"Guess what . . . size doesn't matter.
All firms' clients need your help."
—Todd Bothwell

An unwritten rule of marketing is that you don't want to go fishing for whales in a row boat. By the same token, you don't want to sell yourself short, and never dream big. We are encouraging you to throw multiple irons in the fire, with different expectations of success, and by being both pragmatic and realistic in your expectations, you should be able to develop a business that allows you to capture the low hanging, immediate fruit from point of sale referrals to working with independent agents and brokers, and garnering an understanding of the inner dynamics of institutions of all kinds. These institutions will range from small, medium, and large firms; Partnerships and Professional Corporations, to LLCs and Sole Proprietorships.

Regardless of the actual size of the firm with which you are attempting to forge a relationship, it is critical to remember that you always need the commitment from the owner or owners that they are going to lead the charge in promoting your product or service not only with the clients but also with their employees, especially if this latter group is where the contact with the client actually occurs.

As noted in a previous chapter, another critical component not to be overlooked is the need to obtain approval with the compliance departments of each company and any regulators that regulate the profession of the professional partner. Always start on solid ground before you spend countless hours on building out a successful relationship.

An additional consideration in working with another institution or firm is that they are going to have concerns and questions that differ from yours before they even entertain the notion of you visiting with their clients. These questions may include many of the following:

- Does their contract allow them to work with an outside vendor or professional giving advice to their clients?
- Does their compliance department allow them to receive money from this service in the form of commissions?
- Is each person going to require a life and health license in order to receive compensation?
- How will each of these individuals be appointed? Do they obtain a producer code for your life insurance company through their firm's relationship or directly with your contact at your home office?
- Is this an institution (usually defined as banks, broker/dealers, Registered Investment Advisors, other insurance companies, large financial planning companies, and companies that have publicly traded stock) that wants to partner up with you? If so, be advised that they usually will have several layers of management and you need to find out who you will report to and which person at each office is going to be the person responsible for the success or failure of the new offering.

- What priority will your offering be to the professional partners in that office?
- What is the liability to the company and your professional partner if the service is not offered?
- Will your work efforts and income producing capabilities make a difference to that planner's bottom line?
- How will you keep your offering and the importance of protecting clients in the front of their minds each day and each week?
- How much time will they give you each day; week, month, and year?
- Is this an institution that deals with multiple states? If so, there are licensing issues with most professional partners, so do inquire. Are there different licensing requirements in the various states in which they do business?
- How many employees are going to be involved with you?
- Will there be qualified agents and quality control in place in each state each year?
- How will you handle client referrals in other states? Will your professional partner receive production credit or will the planner in that region where it is sold?
- Who is the ultimate decision maker for marketing the program; for compliance issues, operations issues, sales issues, technological issues, administrative issues and professional partner issues?

The definition of large firms will vary from industry to industry. A large CPA firm may have over $10 million in billable revenues; large brokerage insurance agencies a different metric. Large law firms are usually measured in both the number of attorneys, clients and revenues. Broker/dealers have their own metrics. These firms will also have various ownership structures that address income distributions, equity positions, and management structures.

The two main structures you will run into are:

1. Free Enterprise where owners receive income based on their rain making or business contacts and can achieve high levels of income and success for their effort and contribution.

2. The other is more of a Socialistic equal distribution at the end of the year and no weight is placed on individual contribution.

You need to establish whether every partner and employee is going to be motivated to offer the new service! If so, why, and if not, what needs to happen so that they are motivated to market your product to all of the firm's clients? Sometimes they will have multiple partners and they each serve their own clientele with a servicing hierarchy below them.

Your question needs to be "Are you in business with the entire firm or just one or two partners of that firm?" You want access eventually to all the clients to help them with the issue for which we plan.

Managing partners are common in large firms where one person is responsible for the running of the firm and they usually will poll the other partners to vote on adding new services while weighing the pros and cons to the reputation of the firm and to see if it will derail the focus of the firm. One partner will usually be assigned as the Champion to launch and maintain the relationship for the other partners.

Medium firms (usually 3-10 partners of the types of firms mentioned above and have revenues from $2 million to $10 million) are easier to work with as there are fewer decision makers who get together to decide if offering your new service to their clients is a good idea or not. These firms tend to be in one region or concentrated geographical area and are easier to manage and service. The clients tend to be concentrated in one region as well, but most firms have clients spread out in most states. They may not be big enough to have their own insurance department, and as a result they will often have contacts they refer to for insurance and get paid, while others will strictly refer and not get paid to avoid any conflict of interest. Whether they have their own insurance department or not they still need a planner in senior services to help them with long term care planning; Medicare product questions, Medicaid questions, and other senior product issues/questions each week. Some of these firms are nothing more than a group with a common interest in law; CPA's, financial planning, insurance and others have banded together to share overhead and to provide each of them with other professionals that can take over their clients if they are disabled, ill, die, or will buy them out when they retire.

Partnerships are two people or entities that have decided not to go it alone and to have back up for several scenarios as mentioned above. They can make decisions quickly and will have a pretty heavy client load and their own servicing work structure. You need to inquire to see if one or both partners will be offering the service and if the one partner you are working with exits the business you can carry on with your services for those clients. They may have time and capacity issues as they can only spread the work load off to two people.

Sole proprietorships are interesting as they tend to want to help the clients out with more than one service or they are tunnel focused on one service and have built a business on that one offering. They do it all in terms of compliance, sales, accounting, operations, administrative, marketing, and anything else that needs to be done. Hopefully you will be a breath of fresh air bringing them your work hours at a zero cost to them along with added revenue now and later through policy commission splits renewals. A question to ask is: "How are they going to manage offering another needed service and how much time will they devote to the continuing marketing of your service to their existing clients; referrals, and new clients?" They are quick to make decisions and best of all there are thousands of individuals believing in the American dream waiting to meet you. You may be the difference in them staying in business, expanding their business, or taking their business to the next level. Think about it for a moment. How many people do they meet with that offer to help them increase services to their value proposition, add income to their office now and in the future, at no cost to them, and bring them more clients for their core business?

All things considered, you have expertise that is absolutely critical to our aging Society, and the clients that these financial professionals service. Your primary task is to market your professionalism and product in such a way that you become an invaluable resource to these desired partners.

Chapter Tumblers—Take-Aways:

 Know who your partner is in this undertaking.

 Know who the decisionmakers are, and just how important and what priority your product is to them personally and professionally.

 Know the structure of your partner's firm; be prepared to integrate your services appropriately.

CHAPTER 20

Warm and Target Markets Defined

"It's not what you say, but rather how many
times a day that you say it."
—Todd Bothwell

As the cheese continues to move within the industry and the direct mail lead generation system is replaced by web leads and other social media based systems, changes have been made, not only in the source of leads but also the source of agents as sales leaders begin to recruit with a different strategy in mind. This strategy focus more than ever before requires us to look for people who have warm markets of their own ready to mine as well as target markets which they wish to add to their sphere of influence.

So what is a warm market? A warm, or natural market, is one in which an agent has an existing network of potential or existing clients from which he can extract both selling and centers of influence appointments. When we talk about warm markets we are most commonly referring to people who you know that would listen to you and either help you with your cause to be introduced to others who would want help in preserving their assets/income or people who have similar family values and do not want to burden their family or friends with the responsibility to take care of them as they go through the aging process.

Warm markets are people who share a common interest that you have. So take a look at your life and write down the things you enjoy doing. Let's take skiing or going to plays as a couple of life's fun activities. You would talk to those who you know who go skiing and possibly join a ski club to seek out others that have the same interest and share skiing stories and that will eventually lead you to ask them what profession they are in, giving you the time to discuss the important planning you do for individuals and families. Knowing skiing is an expensive hobby or luxury, most people have discretionary income to fund that sport/activity and they may be candidates to purchase insurance as they would have the money for the premiums. They would also have the ability already to plan for a future event like skiing and would probably have the mind set to plan for a future event such as needing care.

For example, a teacher may naturally gravitate to the educators with whom she has worked in the past and begin to conduct educational group talks, workshops, and small meetings and really trade on the credibility they have by virtue of having taught school. By making use of their past teaching credentials they can empathize with their audience and potential clients, as well as bring credibility to any interaction they might have with district or school administrators. It is a basic rule of marketing that people do business with people they know, like, trust, and relate to on a personal level.

A target market can be a new or desired market into which an agent desires to move the focus of her practice because of a natural attraction or curiosity, as well as aspirations to merely affiliate with this group. For example, if an agent desires to make golf their target market because she has an affinity or passion for the sport, and because she recognizes that golfers reflect the demographics of our average client in terms of health, wealth, activity, education, etc., then this can become a viable market if she follows some simple rules. First, she should always play in a different foursome as this represents a two to three hour period of time during which she will have a captive audience in which to share what she does and how she can be of value to them on a personal level. Second, golf associations and country clubs have a strong affinity with and between their members and should prove to be a valuable source of referrals and a burgeoning network of centers of influence.

A specialty market such as the LGBT (Lesbian, Gay, Bi-Sexual, and Transgender) community can also become either a warm or target market for an agent if they possess the attributes or sponsors necessary to make effective inroads into the community.

The common element in all of these various and sundry markets is of course people. We need to remain client-centric in all that we say and do and provide a level of service that establishes us as the go-to person within our community.

A common misconception that we have to deal with while training our newer agents is that warm market prospecting is not the same as selling Girl Scout cookies to our family and friends. The greatest allure to prospecting in our warm markets is that we *are* talking to people that already know us, trust us, and should be committed to our success, especially if it does not entail their purchasing something from us! We are most interested in who they know and to whom they can make warm introductions on our behalf. By the same token, if you truly believe in your product and services, your friends and family *should* be people that you care enough about to broach the subject of your newly chosen career path.

If that didn't grab you, let us present it to you another way. If you have work done in your home, or see a great movie, eat in a great restaurant, or read a great book, you are naturally inclined to recommend it. Why is this any different? Why does the fact that you are a planning specialist make what you do any less important or significant to the very people that you care most about? In terms of structure, a Project 100 or 200, or list of one or two hundred people who will take your call simply *because they know you* is a natural inroad to our warm market.

Target marketing is different in that you don't usually have these natural contacts that you can reach out to with little fear of rejection. It takes greater effort and commitment in order to crack into a target market. It usually requires the employment of more traditional marketing and advertising techniques.

Another example of a target market that may intrigue you because of a passion you hold for the activity may be attending the theatre or other cultural events. People who attend plays, fine art exhibits/shows, and or symphonies are usually another group that would have the requisite discretionary income to pay for insurance premiums and would see the importance of planning for a long term care event that could occur in the future, just as they have addressed the potential of a fire or burglary that could rob them of something that they treasure as equally as their independence. They see *value* in protecting their investment and the artwork they cherish. The insurance premiums for the insurance riders to insure their expensive paintings or jewelry are *necessary* in their mind. They understand the process of transferring risk to an Insurance company, so they would understand the concept of transferring the risk of long term care costs and the actual care to an insurance company. You can use the above examples to walk through whatever your hobby or interest group may be.

Target markets are different since you are focusing in on many factors in order to formulate strategies to get yourself in the position to meet people who have a need for your service or product. First, you need to decide what geographical area you wish to target and its proximity to where you live as you will be serving this business once you get a mutual agreement from the professional partner you are working with or getting introductions from.

Secondly you need to make sure that a high percentage of the target market will possess the requisite health to qualify for your product.

The third item you need to consider is will they have the discretionary income/money available to pay current premiums and future premiums that may have premium increases over time.

The fourth element you should look at is do they have the mindset or value system that they want to do the right thing and protect multiple generations by transferring the caregiving to non-family members and use an insurance company's money, rather than use their own money to pay for the future costs of care.

The toughest part in getting started will be to select the one area or profession you wish to work with and not get spread out too thin by focusing on more than one area. What we mean is if you are going to pursue financial planners, then it is necessary for you to learn about all the different types of financial planners there are, to wit: fee only based, asset based, insurance based, combination fee and commission and fee—commission-asset based. As you specialize, you will over time have a pulse on the types of financial planners out there and master working with them. For example it would be difficult to master financial planners and estate attorneys as they are different and require different approaches; terminology, and systems and processes.

You will learn tacit knowledge about your chosen profession from the numerous meetings you will have with the planners or attorneys and this will help you break into that specialized market. By learning their terminology and work processes you will be able to further build trust and continue to build meaningful and trusting relationships with them.

> Utilize our "mine your nine" professional partner filtering and evaluation system.

The market is wide open for you to venture out and talk with professionals about using our joint work strategies. Once you select what market to target it gets easier.

By focusing on one profession you are going down the road to becoming a dominant force in your community. We think agents get overwhelmed when they pick more than one type of professional partner and then they shut down and give up working them as they do not have the desired success. Being a jack of all trades and a master of none, leaves you in the position of knowing a little bit about financial planners; some about CPA's, a skosh about benefit brokers, banks, and some about property and casualty offices, but ultimately not enough to be deemed an expert on any one profession.

Another important part of your strategy is going to be determining just how many financial planners or attorneys or professional partners you are going to pursue and keep in your active search. A system Todd created is the "mine your nine" professional partner filtering and evaluation system. It is an approach where we have three professional partners waiting to advance to the next step in qualifying to work with you on a 3-3-3 approach. We meet with nine professional partners and we keep qualifying them to see if they are going to be committed partners and filter them through the coming weeks. You need to continuously rank your nine candidates and see if they are going to rise to your top three. These are three professional partners with whom you will share a large part of your life and work week while helping their clients with long term care planning. It is a spot that is earned and needs to be maintained by the partner since you can always replace one or more of them with the second tier of three professional partners waiting to get moved up. It is important to keep meeting new professionals as you always need to be bringing in new planners to the bottom third so as to constantly have three planners at level one, two, and three. Once you pass nine in the queue, it gets cumbersome to focus on all nine and move them forward. Fewer than nine does not afford you the exposure you need in the community and does not allow you to continue to work with those who really embrace your talents. You will eventually get into a supply and demand rhythm with your time available and they will end up fighting for your time.

The hardest market is of course the cold market in which you have no contacts, no sources of potential introductions, and must rely completely on raw marketing effort.

Marketing and building your personal brand in your community, while work, should be fun and rewarding to you. It should not be drudgery or something that you dread as events and meetings pop up in your calendar. Your warm market provides you a wonderful place to start in terms of growing your confidence, your technical acumen, and will lay the foundation for a strong community network. Don't be afraid to talk to the people you know! You have a great message to share.

Chapter Tumblers—Take-Aways:

 Warm Markets <u>ARE</u> the place to start—don't be afraid to talk to the people you know.

 There really <u>IS</u> an easy way and a hard way—the choice is up to you.

 Marketing should be fun—not drudgery.

CHAPTER 21

The Business Plan

"If all you have is a hammer, everything looks like a nail."
—Bernard Baruch

Up to this point we have determined the "why" and the "purpose" of the partnership. Now it is time to formulate the quantifiable objectives your new partner(s) is/are seeking. Asking questions similar to those asked in the Home Interview with the client makes this a dynamic experience.

In about 30% of the relationships you establish, commission splitting will NOT be an issue. Attorneys, fee-based planners, and other non-licensed professionals will not care about this aspect of the partnership. For those who do, we suggest that the conversation go something like this:

"Jane, in terms of income, just how much money would you like to generate from introducing long term care insurance to your clients?" This is often the moment of truth and this is when you will ascertain her sincerity, level of commitment, and true objectives.

Regardless of the answer, we always then inform her that they will have the ability to earn up to 50% of the production credit or premium, which will then be subject to the commission structure of their personal contract.

Over the years we have worked with any number of producers who have used arbitrary methodology to determine how the production credit will be split between the advisor and planning specialist. We would suggest that you make life easier on yourself, the advisor, and eliminate this stressful aspect of the discussion by simply being honest and forthright and suggesting that the standards of the Million Dollar Round Table (MDRT) be applied to the partnership. Before jumping into that aspect of the negotiations we have found it useful to preface it with a quick review of some basic assumptions that goes something like this:

> "Jane, as I mentioned to you earlier, we have no desire to take your client list. I personally do not like cold calls, I know your clients won't like receiving cold calls, and, upon learning that you gave me their name and number, may take great exception to that and may want to have a few choice words with you. It is a lose-lose-lose proposition, and may even create problems for both of us in terms of violating Do Not Call statutes.
>
> I also want to reiterate that you *earn* your portion of the commission by retaining control of the relationship with your clients. They trust you; they appreciate you, and know that you have their best interests at heart. For this reason we want to become your trusted associate on this one aspect of their financial plan. We don't merely want "access to your book of business" but rather are offering YOU a turnkey marketing system comprised of me, thirty other agents, a General Agent and his staff, as well as a Home Office fully equipped and capable of providing support at every stage of the process to bring this valuable coverage to your clients."

We then suggest that you again confirm what financial expectations that the advisor or firm may be harboring. After they have put this number on the table, you can then proceed to outline the terms of the MDRT program. If we accompany the agent to this interview, the dialogue will often go something like this:

"Jane, as you may recall, there are five aspects to the MDRT Standards for splitting commissions. We have found that utilizing them has made life simpler and more agreeable for everyone.

The first 20% is assigned to the owner of the client. In this case, you clearly own the client relationship and are entitled to this first portion.

Secondly, who is setting the appointment? As I mentioned, your value to our partnership is the ownership of the client relationship. If you are broaching the subject of long term care with your clients in the course of annual reviews, phone calls, and other follow ups, and are the instrument of getting me in front of your client, ideally here in your office so that you can be involved as well, you earn that 20% as well.

The third piece of the puzzle is the actual sale. Now, if you are here in the office, make the introductions, do a review of their portfolio and then excuse yourself while the agent conducts the interview, but come back at the end to validate the plan design and to solidify the sale, we will split this 20% with you, bringing you to 50% of the commissioned sale.

The fourth piece is awarded to the person who is doing the heavy lifting in terms of the application processing, obtaining medical records and completing all aspects of the sales process. This clearly will rest with the agent.

The final piece is awarded to the agent of record who will conduct post-sale activities and additional follow up. Again this will go to the agent.

When all is said and done, you are now 50-50 partners, and you earn your portion by managing your client relations, setting appointments, and facilitating the introductions here in your office. Should you opt to do less than this, we can naturally adjust the split accordingly. So, again, you have the opportunity to earn up to 50% of the sale. Does that sound fair to you?"

We have found that when you position the split in this light, there is no disagreement, and you are still affording them *choice* on how to conduct their business. We would also recommend that you frame up a mutually agreed upon Vision and Mission Statement that adequately portrays your common goals for the partnership. With this plan in place, you can now move on to the Marketing Plan which is critical to all success that you will enjoy in this budding relationship.

Chapter Tumblers—Take-Aways:

 It is important that there just be 'one deal' on the street associated with your agency in terms of commission and premium splits. More than one can be a disaster and ruin your reputation.

 Since many view Money as the root of all evil, it is imperative that you establish a clear understanding regarding the sharing of commissions.

 Other motivating factors may include client retention, asset protection, and the concern for client well-being.

CHAPTER 22

The Marketing Plan

"Vision without execution is hallucination."
—Thomas Edison

The business plan is complete, and you now know that your partner is committed to bringing the protection afforded by long term care insurance to her clients. We know how much money your partner would like to see the partnership generate, and it is now time to get down to brass tacks and to determine the *how* we are going to bring this product to market. Just as we always strive to do with our own regular clients, it is imperative that we are only setting aside our time for quality appointments. By definition, a quality appointment is one in which the client(s) are health and wealth qualified, and eager to see us. In as much as they are working with a financial advisor/ planner or estate planning attorney we can generally assume that the financial aspect of qualification is not an issue. Let's face it; even in the general population lack of financial qualification represents a very small portion of our applicants who do not receive an offer of coverage.

You will have to decide to what degree you want your partner or her staff to pre-qualify the health of your prospective applicants. We would recommend that this review at least cover the "knock out questions" so that you a) don't waste your time or theirs, and b) you walk into the interview with some idea of what products would be appropriate.

The last element, the "eager to see you" part, is completely dependent upon how the interview is positioned by the advisor and how he or she creates the appropriate level of urgency. To this end, *they* have to feel the urgency to have you meet with their clients.

The first logistical challenge is in numbers. First, ascertain how many clients they have, and if an older advisor, how much longer they plan on working? That may sound odd, but the age of the average producer in the industry today is creeping upwards of 58, and managers north of 60. For this reason, you want to do some math together to determine over what period of time you are going to see these people.

Next, do they have clients to be immediately cherry-picked, e.g. ready to purchase, already in the buying cycle, or expressing a pre-disposition to our products because of family experience or their own health concerns.

In terms of organizing the campaign, if they have a sizable base of clients, another way to create urgency is to use birthdays as a trigger for initiating contact with the client. The fact that we can often "save age" on these age attained products is another way to create urgency in both the advisor and the client.

Another means by which to create urgency in the advisor is to demonstrate that we can help them substantiate their ongoing value to their clients and help retain them by being that added dimension of service that can serve to differentiate the advisor from the myriad of other advisors.

It is also crucial to constantly be reminding your partner that you are not a "one man band", and that you actually bring an entire organization to the table with depth in all areas to include, but not limited to, marketing, service, training, compliance, and the capacity to enhance his or her stature with their clients, as well as potential new clients that you both may garner in the course of client appreciation/ referral events.

As the Planning Specialist responsible for the point of sale activity, we cannot emphasize enough the importance of constantly *managing* the relationship. In other words, "out of sight, out of mind" will definitely apply here. You need to have a strong presence in his or her office at the beginning so that the urgency they feel does not wane, just as we have to safeguard that a client's urgency does not ebb and flow as it is prone to do during the buying cycle.

We have endeavored to keep the "How To" of the process simple and straight forward and would encourage you to do the same.

- Keep the process simple and in front of your partner as often as possible.
- Review the desired methodology again and again—it is critical that your partner manage the client relationship—this how he/ she earns his/her portion of the sale.
- Establish a time line of events that need to occur in order for this process to be successfully launched and be replicable on an ongoing basis.
- It is imperative that you completely map out the campaign launch and attach firm dates, especially if the nature of your partner's primary business, e.g. the impact of tax season on a CPA or investment advisor, could be an obstacle to a successful launch.

Final thoughts:

- Communication is always the critical element. At the beginning it will dictate whether you ever get off the ground in your budding relationship. Once you have business in the pipeline, it is important to keep your partner informed during the pendency of the application.
- The key is to get them engaged and the pipeline primed, so a new potential income stream can begin for their business. Additionally, they feel both the gratitude and professional

admiration from their clients as they close this exposed flank in
their financial defenses.

- Working with Centers of Influence is actually an endless source
of referrals and needs to be carefully cultivated and cared for as
one would a fragile garden.

Chapter Tumblers—Take-Aways:

 Over communicate with your partner throughout the entire
relationship.

 These clients belong to your partner. The Partner has always
had all the answers; feed them the information they need to
continue this important relationship.

 Plan the work, and work the plan—often.

CHAPTER 23

Going To Market

"Genius is 1% inspiration and 99% perspiration."
—Thomas Edison

In our experience, the actual marketing of our services to the client is both rewarding and a lot of fun if you establish a plan, and then execute on the plan. These marketing activities can be traditional in the form of letters, e-mails, newsletters, telephone calls, or non-traditional in the form of social events. We would encourage you to really think outside the box and consider activities that have a long "shelf life" and that will help you grow your business exponentially by having your first generation clients become your personal marketers! The key is to adopt a methodology that both of you are comfortable with employing to bring clients in that maximizes the relationship that the Financial Professional has with his clients. Initially it may be by utilizing her ongoing methods of communication to include letters, e-mails, and phone calls, but hopefully will progress to face interviews and appointments [ideally] conducted in the Financial Professional's office.

> We would encourage you to really think outside the box and consider activities that have a long "shelf life" and that will help you grow your business exponentially by having your first generation clients become your personal marketers!—Don Levin

The initial tone utilized by the advisor is critical. He should strive to identify the problem of long term care as it applies to the general public and to the individual client and their family, the inherent risks associated with it, and then propose a potential solution: you. This effort also allows the advisor to create a layer of insulation against potential liability by asking the client for an affirmation that they have been advised about the product and services that you can provide and that they are expressly declining the opportunity to meet with you. A sample letter such as the one found in the next chapter is one that could be utilized. Note: while you can provide this letter as a sample for the advisor to utilize, we strongly encourage you to have it complied not only by the advisor's compliance department but yours as well, given that you and/or your company are being mentioned by name. When in doubt, have it reviewed!

Chapter Tumblers—Take-Aways:

 Think outside the box when it comes to marketing . . . and have fun with it!

 It is imperative that the client relationship be managed by the professional partner.

 All professionals will welcome additional clients—your job is to help them grow their business. Nothing will solidify your relationship quicker than referring them a new client.

Chapter 24

Mechanics of the Marketing Plan

"Every partnership requires either a Managing or General Partner to drive the ship. Accept the fact that in most cases this will be you."
—Don Levin

There is an absolute kaleidoscope of materials available for use in marketing your products. These include Client Letters, Newsletters, Phone Calls, E-mail Drip Campaigns, and our favorite, Marketing Events. The beauty of marketing to our clients and those of our centers of influence and strategic alliance partners is that we can do what we want to do and write it off our taxes.

> "Marketing is nothing more than doing all the fun things that you enjoy and inviting your clients to join you. The best part is that you can then deduct it as a business expense."
> —Don Levin

The keys to any successful marketing strategy are:

- Consistency in both planning and execution. Plan the work and then work the plan.
- Determining a master marketing strategy and establishing a timeline for implementation.
- Develop or acquire materials that suit your marketing purposes.

As we noted earlier, the critical aspect of your professional partner's role is the management of client relations. Ideally the advisor is in regular communications with his client base, and as a matter of course is conveying ideas regarding products, plans, and strategies. Quite often with long term care insurance and similar products they may be at a loss. To this end, a letter such as the following may be a natural way for the advisor to introduce the concept to his clients:

The Initial Client Letter

[Advisor letterhead]

[Client Name] [Date]
[Address]
[City, State, Zip]

Dear [Client]

It is a great pleasure working with you to plan your financial future and to maximize your assets. I feel confident that we have established the financial plan best tailored to your needs and wishes for the years to come.

I have become increasingly aware of the financial and emotional risk facing my clients over the age of fifty . . . namely, the high costs associated with long-term care. Most of us know someone who is receiving care at home, in assisted living, or other long-term care facility. I had hoped the Federal Government would include long-term care in the 1996 Health Insurance Portability and Accountability Act and in subsequent legislation. Some progress has been made in the availability of Partnership plans in the State of Washington, but the accompanying cuts in Medicaid means that this problem largely remains the responsibility of each of us to look out for ourselves.

An increasing number of my clients are concerned about this risk. It was reported by the Federal Government's Agency for Health Care Policy and Research that seven out of ten couples, reaching age sixty-five, can expect at least, one partner to use a nursing home sometime before dying. Depending on where you choose to receive care and the quality of care that you require, the annual cost of an extended stay in a nursing home will range from $80,000 to $120,000 per year! With the stay in care averaging over 2.8 years, this amounts to a substantial investment of your principal investments. Is it any wonder most retirees count outliving their resources as their greatest fear!

A more recent study reports that almost half (48%) of patients currently in skilled nursing homes do not require such a high level of care and need not be in a nursing home! Which brings me to the most important point; the value of assuring one's ability to "age-in-place", stay in the comfort of your own home, avoid overwhelming care giving costs, as well as maintaining choice and control of your own destiny.

After a lot or research, I have found a dependable solution to this problem. I am proud to be able to offer the services of <u>agent name.</u> Mr. / Ms. _____ and his staff of professional long term care specialists know all about the different types of care and the products available that cover this kind of risk. What impresses me most about Don and his staff is their ability to explain the complexities of the plan in understandable terms, as well as to tailor a plan to fit the needs of the people that they are consulting with at that time. After spending some time with Don or one of his associates, you will have the information you need to make an informed decision on whether or not Long Term Care coverage is appropriate for you.

This is such an important issue to you, that I have asked Don to give you a call within the next two weeks to set up a time to meet with you for a Needs Analysis. Everyone associated with Don is a true professional on this subject, and better informed than I am about the options available to cover this imposing risk to your financial future.

Don and his staff have my highest recommendation, and we are proud to consider them as trusted associates in serving you and your needs. You will be able to trust his professional guidance in making the best decision for your particular circumstances. I strongly encourage you to take advantage of this opportunity to safeguard the future of you and your family.

Sincerely,

[Your signature block]

P.S. In the event that you choose NOT to meet with Don or a member of his staff for any reason, please return this letter to me so that we will know that you have considered this advice, and that we may update your file.

TO: [your name]

Thank you for your attention, and kind recommendation to consider long term care insurance at this time. We expressly decline to meet with <u>YOUR NAME</u> at this time to discuss long term care insurance coverage, and understand the potential financial ramifications of this decision.

_____
Client Signature(s)

DISCLAIMER: Remember that this letter is intended for use by the financial advisor or attorney to his or her clients. As a licensed producer, your company or State may prohibit your use of the language found at the end of the letter in which the client is solicited to respond with an affirmative waiver of either purchasing or being exposed to a product offering.

While a letter such as this will provide some level of defense for the advisor, we obviously prefer to be proactive and positive by providing protection to the client rather than merely a "CYA" type letter for inclusion in the client file.

The intent of this letter is to serve as a warm introduction of the concept of long term care insurance, you, and to pivot on the strength of the relationship that the advisor enjoys with her clients.

As previously noted, we also encourage you and your new partner to sponsor joint events to which you can invite your own clients as a sign of appreciation but also to encourage them to bring friends along in hopes of developing even more clients.

We have both been raving fans of client events that are both tokens of appreciation to our existing clients and become referral events by virtue of our clients inviting their friends to accompany them to the event. We both have found that if the venue is a nice restaurant that it is extremely easy to subliminally convince our clients to 'host' their friends at our events. As producers we were both extremely successful at converting these guests into new clients which resulted in hundreds of thousands of dollars of new premium.

Key points regarding client events:

- Think outside the box-in terms of whom you wish to draw, the variety of topics you may wish to offer—keep it fresh for your clients, vary the venue
- Invite clients (to show genuine appreciation) and their friends (growth)
- You want to conduct events that have an extended "Shelf Life" e.g. sushi making, a chef's private table, or golf lessons from a professional. Consider things way outside the box such as an after-hours appraisals and chocolate fountain at a jewelry store, fishing trip, special sporting events, etc.
- Make them fun and memorable so that when people encounter something in their regular life, such as eating sushi, they think of the time that their advisor team created an environment in which they learned how to make sushi.

Key considerations of client events:

- They are a lot of work!
- Consistency and regularity are absolute musts.
- Use a calendar and plan your events out for the next 180 days. Reserve desired venues. Nothing is more frustrating than to have a great idea and to be frozen out of a desired venue.
- If partnering, manage the relationship. Odds are you will have to be the professional planner in the relationship.
- Establish and follow a process and timeline that you can reduce to a checklist.
- Ask your Agency to help promote and support the events.

For agency managers and marketing leaders:

- Plan events that will facilitate the launch of new agents utilizing their Project 100 lists.
- Get involved with your local Chamber of Commerce and host events for fellow chamber members.
- Encourage agents to partner with other agents in your firm, particularly if they have complementary skills to one another.
- Leverage the success of these events to promote more events.
- Get people buying in during the recruiting process.
- Use existing resources as much as possible
- How to drive adoption: agency leaders must "Know it, Model It, and Be Involved"
- First line supervisors must be able to "apply it and monitor it", and the best way to do this is to be modeling the way with your own events.
- As always, a best practice includes tracking activity and success.

Additional Networking Opportunities through the strategic alliance partner

- Who do they know?

- Have them make Personal introductions to their own Centers of Influence that can help you mutually expand your long term care sphere of influence.
- Health Benefits Brokers—the new wave. We have found that this is especially important when dealing in the Business to Business (B2B) arena, where even after you have convinced the decision maker of the business that long term care makes sense for the company and the individual employee, he will often default to "let me check with my benefits person." Rather than being frozen out, it is so much easier if the benefits broker is the one making the introduction and opening the door for you. We both enjoyed success by partnering with a health benefits broker.

Final thoughts on formal and informal marketing events:

- Marketing MUST become part of your lifestyle and DNA, and not remain just a series of separate events in which you occasionally participate.
- Just Do it!
- Face and conquer your fears.
- TALK TO EVERYBODY about what you do! Have FUN!
- Have an elevator speech that flows off your tongue and that prompts questions.

    o "I help people protect their financial futures . . ." How?

    o "I am a long term care planning specialist." What's that?

    o "I educate people on their options for safeguarding themselves and their families against the ravages of long term care and of outliving their money."

    o "I can protect your future."

    o "I help people plan for the events in life that they do not wish to talk about."

Chapter Tumblers—Take-Aways:

 Marketing events create awareness of our products and available solutions; agents complete the sale.

 It all starts with making your elevator speech part of who you are and what you do.

 Say 'thank you' to those you know, and get to know everyone you don't know.

CHAPTER 25

Judo Marketing

"Don't overlook the obvious marketing
opportunities during the workday."
—Todd Bothwell

One of the joys of co-authoring a book is that you get to feed
off of one another, and you never know just what the other guy is
going to come up with when you are brainstorming. This chapter is
one such example. Judo marketing (Todd's term) is where you take the
momentum of being solicited by another business either in the form of
a piece of mail, a phone call or other inquiry, and seemingly with no
effort, read or listen to the message and perform a judo flip and not
only rob the prospector of any momentum but actually turn it around
on them, and prospect them for whatever service or product you are

offering! This is not a customarily used technique, is often overlooked, and we will discuss it in greater detail later in the chapter.

If you have been in sales and marketing any length of time, you know that there are three customary marketing techniques used today. What is common to all three forms is that marketing success is largely hard to measure unless you quantify it by tracking activities and results on a very detailed level. We can say however, that if business is slow you are not doing enough of it!

Seminars

Seminars can educate potential and existing clients about a product or service you are offering. They usually take three months to plan properly and you absolutely need to convert attendees to sales to cover your time, your staff's time, and the expenses of having a proper marketing seminar; unless you are feeling extremely altruistic and don't mind educating the public on your own dime. With proper planning and diligence, your seminar will be the stimulating factor that disturbs the client to action which in turn prompts them to purchase now or in the immediate future. If you do not stay in close contact with them with a steady campaign of follow up communications, your efforts may only serve to reward the next sales person who offers your product or service to the same people. In that scenario, you may have done your job and disturbed the prospective buyer; you just may not get paid for your effort. We recommend you meet with all attendees within two weeks of the event to achieve a higher degree of success.

Awareness Marketing

Awareness marketing is the activity in which you send a letter to a client base or call them and they are made aware of a new product or service. No action is required on the client's part. Unless the client receiving the letter was looking at buying your product and was ready to buy the product, letters usually do not create sales or generate income. This approach is tantamount to

> It's not about the drill bit, but rather, it's all about the hole that they want.

a self-proclaimed effort to keep the US Postal Service in operation. Mailing materials is almost never a winner. Creating awareness today has become one of our greatest allies. As the baby boomer generation continues to age, they also continue to wield tremendous influence as consumers from new car sales to financial services. Nobody *wants* to outlive their money or find themselves in a long term are situation, so making people *aware* of their circumstances, their options, and the products available to meet their needs is what awareness marketing is all about. It's not about the drill bit; but rather it's all about the hole that they want.

Call to Action

Call to action marketing is where you send a communication, letter, email, or phone call, and request the client to take some type of action, such as come into the office for a financial or insurance review. Calls are made for a specific purpose and that is to get an appointment to meet with the client to share a new service; concept, or product.

The major problem we have found through the years is that many professionals like CPAs, insurance professionals, financial planners, attorneys, property casualty offices, benefits brokers, and others were not trained to be seasoned marketing professionals. As a matter of fact few certifications and designations give time or have classes on marketing, yet it is critical for you to expand your reach into the community for more clients once you are established as a prepared planner or sales person. You may be skilled at your craft, but few people know you exist. Does this sound familiar to your situation as a sales or service provider? One of the reasons we wanted to write this book was to get highly trained and skilled planners/agents in front of more families to help prepare for life's challenging events.

Todd started practicing Judo Marketing years ago when he realized that it was expensive to market and hard to measure the success of his marketing dollars. Again, Judo Marketing is where you take the existing momentum of another person and convert that energy into your momentum in trying to help them.

Further explanation: Think of all of those annoying pieces of mail and email communications soliciting your business that you receive. Like most people you may sit by the trash can and throw those pieces away without the courtesy of even slitting them open and peering within them. Stop! Think about what you are doing. You are actually throwing away names and addresses of people who, like you, want to expand their business and have target marketed you, and gone so far as to spend their marketing dollars on you. This is exactly the type of person that would understand you calling them to ask them to sit down with you and let you educate them on what you do if you promise to let them educate you as to what they do.

How does one train their professional partners to be Judo Marketers for your greater common good? Whatever your profession is you need to train the staff and the owners of the business to take the incoming call and solve the issue the person is calling in about, and then add on what you need from them while you have them on the phone, apprising them of a new service or product.

Here is an example on how to perform a Judo Marketing sequence.

A client calls in to a brokerage firm, financial planner's office, CPA firm, Property and Casualty firm, benefits broker, or another professional service. The Judo trained staff answers the phone and answers the incoming momentum call or dishes it off to another Judo trained staff member or possibly shifts it to the Judo trained business owner. The client gets their question answered or problem resolved and the Judo trained staff member then discusses the concern for the client and wants to help them by introducing our new service and possibly the planner that discusses the options of the new service or product. The staff member does this on each incoming call and records the number of calls and families they talk to each week. This is the simplest way to go through the hundreds of clients that are in the data base in a systematic daily work flow until you reach all of the accounts that call in over one year. One of the issues you find in busy, successful, and thriving firms is they are usually at capacity and can't add work flow. They can't add more work to their employee's existing load and the business owner is concerned that we are going to lead them away from their core business. The Judo concept capitalizes efficiently on each incoming call and gives the trained staff the ability to discuss and convey the new service and product to the clients. Then you select the clients that have not called in and then make a plan to systematically call them and introduce them to the new service or offering.

Here is another example of Judo marketing on an incoming solicitation call to the office:

When a sales person calls to sell you something at your office or on your cell phone, this is annoying to most people but actually exhilarating to Todd. Todd talks about training people to lose their fear and calls people each day to talk about our products and services. When someone calls Todd, he always demonstrates the utmost of respect for them and wishes they were working with him. For this reason he will quiz them and ask whether they are satisfied with where they are professionally and whether they get recognition for their efforts. He is looking for people who are hungry and want to work because that is an underlying principle of the American way of free enterprise. When they call you to sell you a service or a product listen to them don't hang up on them and then Judo back to them and tell them what service you provide and how your service can help them; see if anyone in their family has been affected by the lack of your product or service.

We both have infinite respect for anyone that walks in our places of business to sell us something. They have overcome their fear of rejection and grabbed the inner strength to open your door and solicit business. Our staffs know that we want to meet any person who opens our door to sell us anything.

In summary, take all of your contacts each day and just like in Judo shift the momentum of that moment/event and turn it into positive motion to further the momentum for your business.

Chapter Tumblers—Take-Aways:

 Selling is about momentum—it doesn't matter where it originates but rather how you capture it and make it yours.

Be aware of those people who are business-minded enough to be marketing to you and seeking your business for their own.

Take those incoming service calls and convert them into selling appointments for yourself or your partner.

V

INTEGRATION

"If you don't design your own life plan, chances are
you'll fall into someone else's plan. And guess what
they have planned for you? Not much."

—Jim Rohn

CHAPTER 26

Sharing the Wealth

"Let him who would enjoy a good
future waste none of his present."
—Robert Babson

We are both quite often asked any one of the following questions:

- "What can I do with a strategic partner that is not licensed, does not want to get licensed, or may not have any State required Partnership certification completed?"
- "How can I compensate him and/or his firm?"
- "What if I am partnering with an association or other 'entity' that is becoming an endorsement partner for me but does not have the ability to be licensed and appointed?"

- "Is there a way for me to *legally* share some of the proceeds from the sales without jeopardizing my license or my partner's licenses if they do want to share in the pie?"

The short answer to these questions is as follows:

- You may NEVER share commissions with a person, firm, or entity that is not licensed by the State and appointed by your company. Period. Cue heavy boot falling, shaking the ground with great finality, cloud of dust rising dramatically, end of discussion.
- In the event that you and your partner desire for his firm to receive their portion of commissions generated, then the [licensed] partner may assign his commissions to the firm OR the firm may be appointed with the company under the guise of some form of Relationship Marketing Agreement. This agreement still requires an underlying agreement with a member of the firm who is both licensed and appointed. The preceding paragraphs were sponsored by your local Compliance Office.

The dust settles from said boot metaphorically falling and we offer the following alternatives:

- Buy client lists from your partners. Obviously this is contrary to what we have been talking about during this entire book, but this is a legitimate means by which you can provide remuneration to your partners so long as there is a fixed rate per name or list, and it is NOT tied to whether or not a sale is made. To clarify, you *are* buying their client list, but we want them to continue to manage the client relationship. We do not want to be making cold calls!
- Financially sponsor joint marketing events, e.g. you pick up the tab at the restaurant thus establishing a 'savings' for the partner. If your clients become their clients it is often an equal exchange or may be even more lucrative for your partner dependent upon the services contracted for between them and the client.

- Mutual referrals. Some partners will not want to split the proceeds from your sales because they will be deriving proceeds from their own financial product sales or services that you will usually be precluded from sharing in because of your own licensing limitations.
- Another methodology is called "Non-commission fee splitting." These practices may include:

  o Paying to educate their clients [as with an attorney or CPA that is not licensed];

  o Pay to educate their members [if they are part of an association or affiliation.] This can be done by you conducting a workshop or seminar and compensating the association for every person that attends for purely educational purposes.

  o Become a sponsor at one of their events, e.g. a hole of a golf tournament or bowling tournament, or the entire tournament and all of the ancillary costs of hosting such an event.

In any event, don't get caught up in a dollar for dollar accountability. While the MDRT standards previously discussed makes it very simple and forthright when splitting commissions with a licensed partner, the opportunities associated with affiliating yourself with other financial, legal, and insurance professionals is absolutely staggering in scope. A rule of thumb that we have both learned through experience is to be generous in sharing the compensation. We have found that the more you give away, the more you will receive in return.

Chapter Tumblers—Take-Aways:

 You can only share commissions with those who possess the appropriate licenses.

 Joint events keep you on equal ground in terms of expenses and the opportunity to grow your respective practices.

Remaining client-centric is a win-win proposition.

CHAPTER 27

Building a Network

"Are you investing your time or merely spending it?"
—Don Levin

The thing that we enjoy most about marketing is the freedom that it provides us as agents and as sales leaders. Again, when you are not chasing after the lead and going wherever it takes you, you are more in command of your time, your schedule, and your future.

If you are still reading this book, you have obviously established some paradigms surrounding the type of marketing that we have been advocating. Thanks for hanging in there. So the question that we are sure you are asking yourself is "how do I build a network of professional partners that will a) free me up from leads, and b) provide me with a level of activity, i.e. selling appointments, that will allow me to stay as busy as I want to be much less grow my business exponentially.

The short answer is one day at a time, one relationship at a time. While a network is nice, offers flexibility and a deeper and broader pool of potential clients, all it really takes is one or two really committed partners that you can likely stay on top of and fully engaged with. To manage vast numbers of relationships and to see them only once a month would require you to visit more per day than the number of work days that we average in a month. This is not really practical. So what if you had only ten relationships and you met with them every other week? That would mean an average of only one contact per day; totally manageable, effective, and a solid goal to pursue. Remember that regardless of how bright the future looks at the onset of the relationship, if you are not physically present to stir the contents of the pot, you will soon be out of sight and out of mind. The relationship *will* go dormant. This is basic human behavior we are talking about here, and our experiences have certainly taught this lesson time and time again.

One of the more effective networking efforts would involve you establishing a tight network of professional partners that all offer different services that in essence becomes a tightly woven referral system that you own and manage for one another's benefit. This could be a network of professionals brought together such as the ones promulgated by members of the Certified Senior Advisors ® network where attorneys, insurance producers, financial advisors, nurses, mortgage brokers, and other senior-centric professionals band together for the benefit of their senior-age clients.

> "If you are not doing business with your own personal CPA, attorney, insurance agents, it is time for you to replace your CPA, attorney, insurance agents"—Todd Bothwell

So now that we have a quantifiable goal as to the size of the network, where do you find the members of this powerful network? Another simple answer: the Chamber of Commerce, your local NAIFA and FPA chapters, BNI groups, social groups, networking groups, Church, recreational associations, the aforementioned CSA® type of professional societies, or in other words, anywhere you find people.

While a large network of professionals all willingly sending you clients on a weekly basis is a great aspiration, especially if you are a front line leader with agents reporting to you with whom you can share these referrals, remember that we are seeking quality relationships that are based on mutual respect and trust between you. There is no replacement for solid partnerships that are client-centric and always strive to serve the client first and foremost.

The second key to a successful and growing network is to build a solid brand for yourself so that whenever a member of the general public or the professional network that you have constructed, thinks of the product or service you offer, that they immediately think of you. Your name and face should become synonymous with your product or service. This takes time, consistency, and diligence. It does not happen overnight and certainly does not lend itself to the "I tried it once and it didn't work, so I don't ever want to do *that* again" way of thinking. Marketing and building your brand is not an event but rather a lifestyle. Embrace, have fun with it, and then reap the fruits of your efforts.

Chapter Tumblers—Take-Aways:

 Relationships take time to develop and must be nurtured.

 Joining groups is part of the solution and NOT the solution by itself.

 It's about building your brand day by day, week in and week out.

CHAPTER 28

Where to Conduct Business

"Having a diversified portfolio of products and solutions
coupled with many professional partners referring
you clients IS the future of our business."
—Don Levin

We are constantly being asked by our agents where the best place
is to conduct their interviews with the professional partner's clients.
Obviously we are going to do what is preferred by both the partner
and the client, but since we are being positioned as part of their team
as the trusted staff expert/advisor for traditional and non-traditional
long term care, it begs the question that we would want to conduct
the interviews in our professional partner's office unless it is more
convenient and desirable on the part of the client to do so at their
home as we have traditionally. By doing so, we are able to bring the

partner into the interview to "set the table" by doing warm up with the client. This process goes beyond just providing us with a warm introduction and vote of confidence and should usually include a review of the portfolio which provides us with more information for our own interview to follow. Even if the partner then excuses himself to go to his own office to work for 90 minutes while we conduct the interview, so long as he comes back to review plan design and "endorse" the final decision of the client, all the better for everyone. This endorsement is another value added and should be a mutually agreed upon expectation as it will certainly solidify the sale and preclude buyer's remorse from impacting the deal. This arrangement also allows the planning specialist to better trade on the trusted relationship that certainly exists between the partner and client.

Both of us have enjoyed very fruitful relationships with professional partners who have requested that we have a true "presence" in the firm's offices. This has ranged from being included on the firm's website as if a bona fide member of the firm complete with photos, biographical summaries, voice mail boxes and internal e-mails, and titles such as "Director, Long Term Care Insurance" or "Long Term Care Planning Specialist," to carrying business cards that would indicate that we are part of the firm. If pursuing this latter form of affiliation, always consult with your Compliance Department to insure that you are not violating your producer contract's governing provisions on Outside Business Activities (OBA).

We have even been encouraged to foster an image of our presence in the firm by bringing our own personal memorabilia and "wall stuff" if there is an empty office that can be assigned to our use as opposed to our always being in the conference room.

Since the ultimate goal is to be viewed as a trusted part of the partner's team, all of these efforts, as well as attending their client appreciation and referral events, are opportunities for you to build your own brand recognition and reputation. This is networking at its finest!

Being in the office also accomplishes several other key objectives, most notably your ability to "quarterback" the team and drive activity. If you are present in the partner's office, and the word has been put out that you are in fact an equal 'partner' you have the ability to work directly with the staff and drive the activities necessary to conduct successful events which range from the initial contacts, invitations,

RSVPs, follow up, and the subsequent scheduling of appointments. Naturally if you are not present in the office, you will quickly learn that it is most definitely a case of "out of sight, out of mind," and any number of necessary milestones can be supplanted with other 'priorities' that arise. This was definitely our experience even when we were completely immersed in a partnership that successfully generated hundreds of thousands of dollars of premium and commissions. You need to be there to drive activity. Even though it is a partnership in every sense of the word, you will note that in every form of partnership there is always someone identified as either a *General* or *Managing* Partner, and in this instance, it will usually default to you because even in the best of circumstances, you are just going to care more about the success of it than anyone else.

While being in the office of the partner is beneficial on so many levels, it does discount your ability to observe the clients' home life, living style, and does dramatically change the scope of the warm up at the outset of the appointment. This is tempered however by the fact that in some cases you have previously met the client at an event, or alternatively, you can rely on the warm introduction and transfer of trust on the part of your partner.

No matter where you meet, you are still charged with completing your fact finding and analysis, and preparing a plan design and recommendation in terms of product and features that is both appropriate and suitable in terms of meeting your client's needs and wants.

If you are offered the opportunity to have some of your own space in the office of your partner, grab it. If you don't already have an office of your own, it will enhance your professionalism, and your spouse or partner will love the opportunity to rid the house of some of the professional office clutter that you have accumulated over the years.

Chapter Tumblers—Take-Aways:

 In the big scheme of things, it does not matter where you conduct the appointment with the client so long as you do the job!

 The ability to be part of the professional partner's office will enhance your personal professionalism, even if it is only because you have to get out of the house, dress up, and actually become more productive.

 It is still all about the client. By remaining client-centric, you will always come out on top.

CHAPTER 29

Appointment Calendar Management

"The key to multiple client solutions is multiple
client appointments over time."

Todd Bothwell

Managing your calendar and sharing information is the key to being able to have more appointments each week, month and year. The more efficient you are in setting and keeping appointments the more income you will earn each year. Your partner will probably already understand this concept, but in the event he or she does not, you may have to demonstrate for her the importance associated with calendar management. Keep in mind that some professionals *fully* understand the significance of time accountability. Attorneys more often than not bill in six minute increments as they represent 1/10th of one hour.

The conversation may very well be part of the business plan development when you determine based on desired income goals that they express, just how many applications will have to place, how many applications will have to be submitted, and therefore how many appointments have to be successfully seen and closed.

A positive aspect of working with a partner who has a close knit client base is that as your selling appointments go up in volume and successful completion, you will in turn meet more people and help more people get the product or service you offer.

Even if you work a five day work week, most agents can successfully complete three appointments in a day and not be mentally exhausted and therefore still possess the ability to be "on" for the next day's three appointments. At first it does not sound like much of a problem to keep up with, but as you add follow up appointments, e.g. where you see the clients a second time or you add annual reviews into the mix the calendar can become quite cumbersome to manage if there is not a system in place.

When other offices are booking appointments for you they need to view your calendar as well to see when you are going to be available. They also need to allow for you to rest between appointments or drive time between appointments. They should allow rest room breaks; meal breaks and breaks to return calls and emails. You, or your appointment setters, should provide you with ½ hour windows as well to give you time if you run into traffic; unforeseen problems, or appointments that simply run longer than expected.

The capacity for the maximum number of appointments per week will vary from agent to agent, and be dependent upon how many segments of the day the agent will work or wants to work. For all intents and purposes, each day has three segments: morning, afternoon, and evening. If you work the full work week Monday through Friday, that would give you 15 appointment capabilities per week. [Note: if you are basing yourself in a partner's office or conference room and the clients are coming to you rather than you traveling to them, the number of appointments you can see increases significantly in a shorter period of time, e.g. purely regular business hours, and you can become quite efficient at seeing people while still remaining fresh and free from the stresses associated with travel in metropolitan areas.] If you took one appointment in the morning; one in the afternoon and one in the evening you would be a very successful agent. Agents who are focused on attaining high status in terms of production or the shattering of sales records, and that have the energy to exceed and go to the next level, will push themselves and often work Saturdays in order to potentially achieve eighteen plus appointments a week. Scheduling an abundance of appointments allows you to take those occasional cancellations or postponements in stride, and still put up a solid week's worth of production.

In the event that you have multiple professional partners that are working with you, it is imperative that you create some form of electronic calendar available online that they can all immediately access so as to allow them to book appointments without conflicting with others also being placed into your calendar. Some of the choices for a calendar management tool would be Yahoo or ATT calendars where more than one office can set appointments for you. The key is for you to maintain as complete a calendar of your own appointments as possible to include such things as family obligations, personal appointments (i.e. medical and dental), vacations, continuing education, agency meetings, marketing appointments, as well as anything else that is a demand on your time. Things will definitely get more involved as you become more successful each year and calendaring will get really interesting when you start offering additional products to your clients that require multiple appointments in order for you to be able to prepare necessary quotes and fact sheets.

> A lawyer's [Long Term Care Planning Specialist's] time is his stock and trade." Abraham Lincoln

It is no secret that we are striving to get away from the transactional (one sale) mindset and to adopt a relationship mindset that encourages the existence of five or more product offerings per household. In other words, you will be more efficient, and your client base more robust if you are selling five products to one household rather than one product to five households.

As you become more proficient, you will achieve no less than a fifty percent closing rate in your appointments. Taking the long view, this means that if you are successful in setting (or having them set for you) 12-15 appointments per week, this will equate to 6-7 sales per week which in turn means between 300 and 350 sales per year! In the event you are in fact selling more than one product to your clients, this number can grow even more significantly. If your quiver of arrows includes long term care insurance, annuities, Medicare product policies, and life insurance, you will find that the number of appointments that you actually complete may become a bit fuzzy, but at the same time, you will not be faced with the pressure of having to conduct so many first time appointments. Often, agents working lead programs were accustomed to selling new clients each week and not having a relationship thru which they could sell more than one product to them. Usually this was by their own design, though it could have been that they were in fact limited by a either formal or informal direction not to cross sell products due to contractual limitations.

Conversely, if you are in a sales position and only able to achieve 2-3-4 selling appointments each week you are in a vicious cycle of frustration that prevents you not only from achieving the earnings you are seeking but also prevents you from building the momentum and competencies that will ultimately inhibit your closing and placement ratios. A simple rule of thumb is that the busier you are, the more momentum you have, and the more confident in your capabilities you will become. This momentum is both contagious and as habit forming as a narcotic. Top producers will tell you they thrive on days that are jam packed with appointments, because "it is show time" and that they "get up for big game days." Other analogies that are applicable would include viewing yourself as a Top Gun pilot or actor. As a Top Gun pilot, you are catapulted off the aircraft carrier in a rush of adrenaline and steam to fly your mission, and when you return after the mission, and your tail hook captures one of the trapping wires, you are absolutely the best. As an actor/performer the curtain goes up or the cameras start to roll, and you find yourself completely engaged in delivering the performance that is going to win you the next Tony or Oscar. Some top producers book heavily 3 days a week and literally rest the days between. Professional athletes get up for the big games and top producers get up for the big appointment days.

There can be different types of appointments each day depending on how you operate. There are the first client appointments where you design plans, get to know clients, fill out your fact finders, or gather and write applications. There are second appointments where you did not have time to complete the sale or the client needed time to discuss their options together in private. There are annual client reviews where you remind the client why they protected their future and transferred the risk to an insurance company or update their policies with current coverage values. So a busy agent will have several different types of appointments each week. If they sell more than one product they can book appointments in advance like dentists book teeth cleanings in advance.

Todd came up with the realization while sitting in his dentist's office a number of years ago, that we could all learn quite a bit from our dentist. Not only does he or she have a staff that actively manages his or her calendar, as a business developer our hats are off to this professional. Consider this scenario and evaluate the merit of this argument. You visit your dentist's office for your semi-annual exam and cleaning, and what happens during this appointment? First, they take an x-ray and have a dental technician poke around in your mouth with a steel instrument looking for decay; then the dentist comes in to the exam room to evaluate the results and you hold your breath waiting for the verdict. "Well, we need to replace those metal fillings, and I am concerned about these cracks in your teeth. The sensitivity you are experiencing is the result of this and that; and these other issues will require an additional appointment. Even with what may turn into a prolonged treatment plan, they will nonetheless still remember to schedule your next semi-annual visit! Sheer genius. Then they give you a plan of treatment and the estimation of costs on each tooth. Like root canal on #12; replace fillings on # 6 and on # 11, crown needed on #10, sensitivity on #13 could be another root canal from infection in #12 not sure, and so on. Total projected costs: well, better that we don't burden you with that pain too. They now have us coming back for the next several months to fix the problems one at a time and spread the costs over a longer period of time. The beauty of the dentist marketing his services to clients is it is systematic and each day they walk in to work they have some first time appointments; second appointments, as well as those very lucrative semi-annual exams and cleanings.

If you will mirror the concept of the dentist and instead of an x-ray fill out the fact finder and lead with the financial service that is the most pressing for the client, whether an annuity, life insurance, long term care, Medicare product policy, disability policy, or other service or product you will be successful. Just like the dentist doesn't fill your mouth with Novocain and perform all the dental treatments in one day due to pain and client inability to pay all at once, you can spread the appointments over a period of time as well and handle one client need and one policy at a time. Prioritizing what needs to be done first and establishing the treatment plan for the next several months or even years also allows for spreading out the financial burden for the client and allowing the client to understand transferring the risk one appointment at a time. Just as we would not want our dentist to complete a plan requiring extensive work all in one day, financial services clients often need it spread out over several appointments to avoid feelings of confusion or of being overwhelmed. Focusing on one product per appointment is a good rule of thumb. However, this will often require you to keep following up and gently pushing them forward.

In summary, whether you are selling one or multiple products, you need a great calendar management system. If you are working with several professional partners they need access to your calendar to set appointments for you to book your week/month solid. It is completely acceptable to book appointments far out into the future so long as you have a reminder system to frequently send an email to the client that jogs their memory, again, just like our friend the dentist.

With luck, you will have many professional partners which include multiple CPAs; health insurance agents, attorneys, insurance brokers, benefits brokers, property and casualty offices and others that are all trying to book one of their clients to meet with you and are literally fighting for one of your fifteen available appointments each week. They should view you as a rare commodity with expertise that their clients desperately need in order to safeguard their futures. It all begins with how you view yourself!

Chapter Tumblers—Take-Aways:

 Top producers are great sales people but also masters at calendar management.

 The more professional partners that you have referring clients to you the more important calendar management becomes.

Different types of appointments will require various lengths of time; proper calendar management will prevent valuable appointment slots from being squandered.

CHAPTER 30

Exponential Growth

"You can hit the flywheel with multiple solutions per client and multiple professional partners sharing and referring clients with you."
—Todd Bothwell

Exponential growth comes at the end of the process of pursuing multiple professional partners with common beliefs and goals; working your existing clients for multiple line sales, and helping clients solve for more than one financial solution in their life.

After implementing a system of exponential growth by leveraging your time and effort, there may come the realization one day that makes you sit up and take stock, "Hey I am starting to get really busy". In business you can do all the work yourself and put in all the hours yourself and that is called linear work. There is a finite level to the success that you can achieve, and this usually translates into a cap on your potential income. Don hit this as an attorney when he was once again working on his own, and a shrewd legal headhunter pointed this out to him and suggested that changing the breadth of his practice was his only option if he wished to make more money for his family. We call this linear limitation, the firm of "Me, Myself, and I." When you expand and you have several people setting appointments for you, referring clients to you, and marketing your services to their own clients that sets the stage for what we refer to as exponential growth.

Think of Todd's friendly dentist again and whether he just does fillings or is content with a one product line of sales. Would such a dentist that only fills cavities stay in practice very long? Highly unlikely. Would you want to have that dentist as your practitioner (unless you had a lot of cavities)? Again, unlikely. As a result, you seek out a dentist that takes care of all of your dental needs, ranging from the six month teeth cleanings, veneers, root canals, teeth whitening, as well as those cavity repairs. As you would suspect, this dentist undoubtedly makes more money and helps more people. This is no different than the planning agent—You—who helps the client protect his independence and financial wellbeing with the purchase of long term care insurance, helps create wealth with an annuity, and creates security for the family by creating a layer of protection in the form of life insurance.

You can also show concerned parents how an income rider annuity for stabilizing a predictable income stream for the portfolio to assure certain staples like the house payment and car payment are made each month. You can hit the "Fly Wheel" and get in your groove and do planning every day, and with them in turn becoming part of your marketing and brand building strategies, leverage yourself so you in turn have more people who want to see you next week than you had the week before. You are even more effective in working smarter, not harder.

This sounds simple, and like something that we should all want to embrace, yet, something prevents us from doing it. We have determined that some people have a fear of success because once this happens they have to work hard every day and for a long uninterrupted period of time with few days off. Especially those who value time off more than earning more money or controlling their pace of work and number of hours they work each week. The focus on getting one or two appointments a week referred to you from other trusted advisers can really add up. It is interesting how a good partner will talk about having you as his/her exclusive planning specialist because they understand the significance attached to the numbers of you meeting with their clients not only from an income standpoint but also in terms of logistics. You may have to point out to them that meeting with only two clients a week for 50 weeks during the year will only allow you the ability to assist 100 clients a year; if they have 1000 clients it would take you a total of 10 years to meet with all of the clients.

Another important item we identified while working with CPA and Law firms was to be aware of just who you will be working with when you sign up a firm in which all partners, managers, and employees may or may not be referring business to you. You may sign up a firm that has 5000 clients but if you only have one partner working with you and introducing you to his clients you really only signed up a 500 client firm with nine partners who do not have the time, capacity, or belief to work with you. Once all partners get engaged and see the value you bring to the clients and their core business they will jump on board, especially if the managing partner is a leader and endorses you and enforces that we will get these families covered.

The sky is the limit with the number of professionals who are out of time, at capacity, do not have the selling skill set, want to retain clients, want to add value, and would like to have a continual residual income into their retirement. Your charge is to find them!

Having a diversified portfolio of products and solutions as well as many people sending you business each week is the future of our business. You really need to work your book of business going forward and spend time networking and doing marketing activities like group talks, client appreciation events, and media events, in order to build a sustainable business. We suspect that many agent retirement parties will be prematurely happening if people will not change, and really get back to putting in the hours needed in to win in the new business model ahead.

Chapter Tumblers—Take-Aways:

 Working by yourself, e.g. setting your own appointments is purely linear. Exponential growth occurs when others are filling your appointment pipeline.

 Multiple insurance solutions provides you the capability of multiple appointments and potential sales.

 Fact Finding will take on incredible significance to you as you exponentially sell more products to more clients.

CHAPTER 31

Social Media

"If there is a better way to do it better . . . find it."
—Thomas Edison

A final thought on how to grow your business: Social Media. While referrals and warm introductions remain a great way to reach one client at a time, imagine having the ability to reach hundreds, if not thousands, at a time. What would this ability do to your business? Imagine being able to get your message out to this many people in one fell swoop. The opportunities remain endless.

It is probably fair to say that we all now rely on the Internet when we begin our search to buy something new, ranging from cars to other commodities. For this reason it is important to remember that people obtain information, news, education, and other pertinent data from both electronic and print media as they ponder planning for their purchases.

By definition social media includes sites such as Google, Facebook, Twitter, LinkedIn, as well as any and all other mediums that are available to reach large (or small) numbers of people. While print advertising is largely an archaic method, the aforementioned social media outlets, as well as cable television, provide the ability to really focus in on your target audience. This is a tremendous opportunity and can be a very economical alternative to the traditional media outlets. The most telling characteristic of social media outlets is the ability to reach small or large audiences with specific messaging by choosing the channels and their associated audiences, e.g. gender, age, occupation, etc.

Social Media technologies provide the advertiser with the ability to provide scale to his efforts and to target specific segments of society for products such as long term care by focusing on the channels selected for the campaign. Also in your control is the number of times that your ad is displayed and the messaging that is employed.

Social Media has also impacted how companies build their brands, launch their new products, and communicate with the public in general. While this is an exciting alternative, the key is to integrate it into your overall marketing plan and, as with everything else we have been talking about, maintain consistency in its use and application.

Up until now, most of us have not taken advantage of social media to grow our respective practices and agencies, but that is changing right now. We must all, embrace the changes that have and are taking place and implement them into our ongoing marketing plans.

This too is the future of our business.

Chapter Tumblers—Take-Aways:

 Social Media is here, it's now, and we all need to embrace it!

 Make it part of your marketing plan and the building of your brand.

It can be the key to your success in getting your message out so that people will know who you are, and what you can do for them!

VI

POSTSCRIPT

"Winning takes talent, to repeat takes character."
—John Wooden, UCLA Men's Basketball Coach

"I used to want the words 'She tried' on my
tombstone. Now I want 'She did it.'"
—Katherine Dunham

POSTSCRIPT

"Before enlightenment, chop wood, carry water. After
enlightenment, chop wood, carry water."
—Zen saying.

This book has been a labor of love as we have simply let the
chapters write themselves. We have spent time reflecting on what
has been successful for us and our agents over the years versus the
things to avoid in the future. We have reaffirmed for ourselves and to
one another that our best days as sales leaders and for our producers
remain ahead. We are a part of a tremendously vibrant industry, and
the opportunity to live a life of significance has never been greater as
we make a huge difference in the lives of our clients. The advent of
additional product lines with which to meet the needs of our clients on
a more holistic basis coupled with a market that is growing faster than
we can service it as clients continue to get younger and younger when
purchasing our products makes it a matter of using the talent that each
of us possesses, coupled with the passion and compassion inside of

each of us, to be able to succeed in helping more and more people. We make our successes replicable because of our character.

First and foremost it has to be all about the clients. When we place their interests first, foremost, and always, the by product is that we are in a position to truly 'do good' and to live a life of significance by making a difference in the lives of others. Not only do we achieve a professional high, but we are also financially rewarded for our efforts.

We both now have children of our own working in our respective agencies. When we are asked by a prospective agent in the course of the selection process just how much we believe in what we do, and what their potential for success is in today's market, all we can do is humbly point to a picture of our respective son or daughter, and allow their presence to speak volumes about our passion for what we do every day. We hope that all of you feel the same way about what you do each day, and that you recognize that each day is about the Journey and not the Destination. Having a client go on claim because they now need assistance with the activities of daily living or are suffering some form of cognitive impairment, is truly a memorable experience. Like a police officer who never draws his gun, some agents will never experience a claim. Fortunately or unfortunately, our first claims occurred only shortly after our entry in the business. We still get emotional when we recount our independent yet common stories. When you tend to these people much like a shepherd tends his flock, there is no greater reward except maybe when a client has died and you have both the opportunity and privilege of delivering the death benefit on a life insurance policy that allows a family some degree of continuity and normalcy, despite the loss of a loved one especially if that person was the primary breadwinner. We truly make a difference.

Everything that we have written about in the course of this work is something that we have lived, breathed, and implemented as we plied our craft within any number of markets across the country. All of the strategies work *if they are implemented*. It is all about active marketing, building your brand, networking, and prospecting a dominant portion of your professional life. One and done won't work. It is a lifestyle, not an event.

What we do is important work, and as Ken Blanchard and Sheldon Bowles related in their bestselling book *Gung Ho!,* It is all about the Spirit of the Squirrel (worthwhile work), The Way of the Beaver (in control of achieving the goal), and the Gift of the Goose (cheering others on). This can be a lonely business—agents can be made to feel like the proverbial Maytag Repairman—but both of us have been fortunate to be part of organizations that permit our agents to work on their own without being alone. The concept of "reach one, teach one" has always been prevalent in our company's culture, no matter the change in entity, organization, or challenges hurled at us by our industry as veteran agents embrace newer agents, teach them the attributes of our culture, and raise up another generation of planning specialists.

Whether working as an executive on Wall Street, working with CPA and law firms, working with his own long term care clients or working with agents as a General Agent, Todd has learned that all clients in all states have similar issues in that they will all age and need some form of help later in life. Our job is to help them accept this fact.

Many of the agents in these various regions also had the same issues in terms of fear of the unknown and realizing their job had changed quickly from meeting with people that had an existing interest in long term care planning to marketing and finding people and developing an interest in long term care planning. Todd wants to thank those agents that made the effort to join me for hours in professional partner meetings and 'drop-ins,' as well as the time spent in the car as we ventured into the unknown of marketing and building relationships for future business. This activity has been a large part of my life for the majority of my professional career. Pursuing professional partner relationships and the hunt for new clients through referrals, seminars, and by living each day telling everyone that I meet what I do has become a way of life. Watching agents cross over and making the decision to go tell others in their community what they do and why they do it is really rewarding to me. The biggest opportunity now is to not only tell the professional community what we do, but to learn and offer clients multiple solutions to prepare them for a long retirement not only with long term care planning, but income planning, life insurance planning, and consistent long term asset growth.

Don, and his agents, most recently, in the Pacific Northwest Agency, adopted the identity of the Wolf Pack; not solely because it fit the geography of the agency, but because Rudyard Kipling so eloquently summed up the purpose of their existence in his *The Second Jungle Book:*

Now this is the Law of the Jungle—as old and true as the sky;

And the Wolf that shall keep it may prosper, but the Wolf that shall break it die.

As the creeper that girdles the tree-trunk, the Law runneth forward and back—

For the strength of the Pack is the Wolf, and the strength of the Wolf is the Pack.

THANKS AND ACKNOWLEDGMENTS

To Susie Levin and Susan Bothwell, our wonderful wives, for supporting the idea, offering editorial critiques, and painstakingly proof reading several drafts of this work, and allowing us the time to write on our own and with one another.

To Jeff Levin, for succinctly providing us the tag line to for this book "Unlock Your Future through Marketing."

To all of our agents and second line leaders, for having the trust and confidence in us, thus allowing us to play mad scientist and to experiment with various and sundry marketing techniques with them.

To Bill Nelson for being a willing set of extra eyes and a great proof reader and source of objective commentary, while enduring multiple reads. Thanks Bill.

To Lisa Resnick and her staff for supporting the idea of this book and providing us a forum in which our voices could be heard.

To Lisa Resnick, Craig Halverson, James and David Berwick, Carrie Murray, Janet Greiling, Tara Simmons, Bill Nelson, and Jeff Levin for taking the time to read the book and offer industry insights.

Thanks also to the agents of the original Dog Team and Wolf Pack in Chicago, the Cincinnati Royals, the Mighty Northeast Express, the Virginia Wolf Pack, and the Pacific Northwest Wolf Pack who bravely allowed Don to make those teams, large and small, extensions of him as he experimented with these marketing tools. You know who you are.

To the agents of Great Lakes, Mountain West, and Southern Plains, Todd sends a big thank you for having the faith to follow him and to let his many years of "hands-on" field experience guide them to comfort and success in their own marketing endeavors. You remain a constant in his passion to further the long term care insurance industry.

To all of you who each and every day strive to do right by your clients, and to offer them solutions rather than product with the proffer of an intangible promise to be there in the future when care is needed.

We would also like to thank all of the various professional and strategic partners with whom we have worked, for their trust and confidence in allowing us to work with their clients, as well as to serve these people and their families.

As Rosalynn Carter once said:
"There are four types of people in this world:
Those who have been caregivers,
Those who currently are caregivers,
Those who will be caregivers,
And those who will need caregivers."
We would like to think that the great long term care planning specialists with which we have had the privilege to associate over the years have made a difference, and maybe, just maybe, became a fifth

type: those who provided the plans and hope for the future to the families of those who ultimately required care.

Don Levin

Todd Bothwell

ABOUT THE AUTHORS

"What really knocks me out is a book that, when you're all done reading it, you wish the author that wrote it was a terrific friend of yours and you could call him up on the phone whenever you felt like it. That doesn't happen much, though."
—J. D. Salinger, *The Catcher in the Rye*

Don Levin
JD, MPA, CLF˚, CSA˚, LTCP, CLTC
General Agent
Genworth Financial Agency, Inc.
Pacific Northwest Office
2012 Platinum Agency
2013 Platinum Agency
2013 First in Class—GAMA International

Don has been in the long term care industry since 1999 during which time he has been an Agent, District Leader, Marketing Leader, Regional Sales Manager, Associate General Agent, and Divisional Vice President. Don is also a former practicing Attorney-at-Law, court-appointed Arbitrator, as well as a retired U.S. Army officer.

In addition to his various Law and Life & Health insurance licenses, Don has earned the Chartered Leadership Fellow˚ (CLF˚) professional designation from The American College, as well as the CSA˚, CLTC˚, and LTCP designations. He has also earned Green Belt certification through GE's Six Sigma program, and is a graduate of GAMA International's Essentials of Leadership and Management. He has also taught *Managing Goal Achievement˚, Integrity Selling˚* and *The Way to Wealth˚* to hundreds of leaders and salespeople over the past thirteen years.

Don earned his Juris Doctor from The John Marshall Law School, his MPA from the University of Oklahoma, and his BA from the University of Illinois-Chicago. He is also a graduate of the U.S. Army Command & General Staff College and the Defense Strategy Course, U.S. Army War College. Don previously possessed FINRA Series 7, 24, and 66 licenses as well as Real Estate Sales and Brokers licenses.

In his spare time, Don is an author, and has published eight books in a range of genre. Don is very active with his church and within the community, and remains focused on his wife Susie, their five children, thirteen grandchildren and two dogs aptly named Barnes & Noble.

Other titles by Don Levin available at www.donlevin.com include:
The Code
Knight's Code
Broken Code
The Leader Coach: Exposing Your Soul (with Terry Edwards)
The Gazebo: The Life Story of Holocaust survivor Alexander Lebenstein (with Alexander Lebenstein)
Eight Points of the Compass: Directing Our Children on the Path to a Better Life
Don't Feed the Bears: How Parents Can Set Their Kids Up for Failure
Wisdom of the Diamond: The Five Bases of Effective Team Leadership (with Tom Bartosic)

Todd D. Bothwell
MBA, CLU, ChFC, CLTC
General Agent
Genworth Financial Agency, Inc.
Southern Plains Office

Todd started working in the financial services field at the age of 12 in his father's financial planning firm. In 1977 he opened a property and casualty office and then a real estate company, all while attending college at the University of Arizona. It was here that Todd began integrating life, disability, and property and casualty insurance sales with the same customers. Todd then worked as an Investment and Insurance advisor in a Regional Bank. Once again integrating insurance, investment, and banking product sales with the same customers.

He then moved to Atlanta, Georgia where he was the District Manager for a major life and securities corporation. Later he became a partner in an Estate Planning Management firm. He started offering long term care insurance plans as part of asset preservation for the comprehensive estate planning process. Additionally, Todd was an adjunct professor at Oglethorpe University teaching the Certified Financial Planner curriculum.

Todd was then recruited to be the Managing Director of a large securities broker dealer specializing in large CPA and Law firms. In that role he helped create and pioneer the integration of offering financial planning products to the firm's clients. He was instrumental in creating a new revenue source for the firm and subsequently recruited, hired and trained financial planners to integrate with the firm's clients.

After a successful turn at the broker-dealer, Todd was invited to become the Executive Vice-President for a professional money management firm. He was brought on to educate and recruit CPA and Law firms to integrate professional money managers into their firms in an effort to help clients with individual designed portfolios tailored for their risk levels and goals.

Todd returned to work in the long term care and senior market, where he enjoyed the agents and the clients. That change brought him back to Genworth Life Insurance Company as a managing General Agent. In that role, he recruits, trains and manages agents in cross selling multiple products, while teaching referral training as well as building relationships with professional partners to create referrals. This is Todd's true passion, which he has refined over the past 36 years.

Continually in pursuit of advancing his education, Todd earned a BS in Business from the University of Arizona, and holds a Master's in Business Administration from the University of Phoenix, and has obtained the Certified Long Term Care designation, the Chartered Life Underwriter® and Chartered Financial Consultant® designations from American College. Previous designations and licenses held but not active are: CFP, CSA, AIF, FINRA series 7 and 24 and 65.

Todd is married and resides in Edmond, Oklahoma. He has four children and five grandchildren.